A Promise
to America

——God's Guarantee——

CAROLYN CORBIN

PenPoint Press / AUSTIN, TEXAS

People's names used in this work are fictitious except for those of my cousins and aunts who have granted, or if deceased, their relatives have granted, permission to use their real names. Except for my relatives, any names used in this text, if associated with someone or with a particular event or circumstance, will be purely coincidental.

Scripture quotes are from the Holy Bible, King James Version.

FIRST EDITION
Copyright © 2003
By Carolyn Corbin
Published in the United States of America
By PenPoint Press
A Division of Sunbelt Media, Inc.
P.O. Drawer 90159 ✑ Austin, Texas 78709-0159
email: sales@eakinpress.com
💻 website: www.eakinpress.com 💻
ALL RIGHTS RESERVED.
1 2 3 4 5 6 7 8 9
1-57168-806-4

To all Christians in America.
You are on a co-mission with God to heal our land.

Other books by Carolyn Corbin:

Strategies 2000

Conquering Corporate Codependence: Lifeskills for Making It Within or Without the Corporation

Great Leaders See the Future First

Contents

Foreword by John A. Weber   vii
Preface   ix
Acknowledgments   xi

Section 1: *America's New Challenges*

Chapter 1: Christian Responsibility   3

Section 2: *God's Requirements for Healing the United States of America*

Chapter 2: Humble Yourself   13
Chapter 3: Pray   25
Chapter 4: Seek God's Presence   39
Chapter 5: Focus on Godly Obedience   49

Section 3: *God's Promises to the United States of America*

Chapter 6: God Hears Our Prayers from Heaven   63
Chapter 7: God Forgives   71
Chapter 8: God Will Heal Our Land   89

Foreword

You hold not a book but a special treasure from God. Carolyn Corbin writes with uncommon insight, in beautiful prose, and with a heart turned to Christ. Carolyn and her work are genuine gifts for the rest of us to enjoy and savor.

I'm a Carolyn Corbin junkie. Her writing and speaking always challenge and minister to me. Maybe it's because Carolyn's roots are deep in the soil of North Texas farm life. Or that her experiences, broad reading, and solid educational background have given her a keen perception of life in the third millennium. Or that she has a spiritual center to her life that guides her clearly and consistently. Perhaps it is because she tells great stories with a warm sense of humor. For these reasons and many more, I listen to everything Carolyn says and read everything she writes.

Solid Biblically, culturally insightful, and an open window to Carolyn's heart are qualities that mark *A Promise to America: God's Guarantee*. Visiting with key leaders and considering important issues in science, industry, education, and sports gives Carolyn critical insight into the challenges of our day. Courageously she tackles tough and critical issues that others avoid—issues like ethical relativism, spiritually impoverished values, and the need for Godly leadership. She applies the Words of Christ as well as the Work of Christ and finds wonderful answers and workable solutions to current problems and challenges.

Carolyn's book will lead you to a deeper Biblical understanding, greater cultural comprehension, and increased spiritual commitment. Read it. Digest it. Apply it. This work is a wonderful gift from a gracious Heavenly Father. Carolyn and her husband, Ray, are friends, examples, and spiritual leaders for me and my family.

Carolyn, THANK YOU for your special friendship. You are one of the best!!

— JOHN A. WEBER
Dallas Cowboys Chaplain

Preface

Dear Fellow Christian:

We live in challenging times. Never in global history has there been so much unrest and chaos. As globalization brings nations face to face with one another and introduces the world to new cultures, change is taking place at a rapid rate. The ideal vision is that people in the world will be able to live together and share a common bond of peace and prosperity. The hope is that a majority of nations will participate in world trade, and the economies of once poor nations will be productive and prosperous. As nations are entering new markets, becoming democracies, aligning in global politics, and finding their places in this new world, chaos has broken out and threatens world stability. This is a predictable model in that chaos always accompanies change.

However, chaos can be very dangerous. Much disruption can take place before moving through it to the other side wherein peace can reign. Weapons of mass destruction in the hands of despots destined to do harm endanger global stability. The United States of America, our beloved land, is a target for terrorists and rogue nations who wish to destroy our freedom and disrupt our economy.

As we move through this global turbulence, we need God's protection. Great wealth and the mightiest, most high-tech military in the world are not enough. God must be in the details. In order to protect and heal our nation, God puts the responsibility on Christians.

He promises to heal our land if we will exercise His prerequisites. He lays out these requirements in 2 Chronicles 7:14.

Every Christian has a part in God's work. Our lives have eternal purposes. In effect, Christians are being asked to change the world. And changing the world carries with it a massive responsibility. In fact, it is a daunting task. The very idea seems too big to ponder. But it can happen one step at a time, one life at a time.

We are on a co-mission with God. He has continuing work to do and is depending on us to carry out His tasks that lie ahead. Too often we feel that we should start outside the Christian community to correct national problems, but this verse clearly indicates that God's people—today that means Christians—are the ones who must demonstrate faith in Him and exercise specific behaviors before He will protect and heal our nation. What an awesome responsibility!

My goal for this work is that, as you read this book, you will renew your relationship with Jesus Christ and practice the process of actualizing your faith—first, because God wants it to happen, and second, because it has a direct effect on the future of America.

God bless your journey.

— CAROLYN CORBIN

Acknowledgments

It is impossible for me to write a book without encouragement from many friends, coworkers, and family members. Producing the work is always a team effort.

Special appreciation is extended to Euna Brady, who spent many hours proofing the manuscript and making suggestions for improvement. Euna is a loyal friend and coworker.

Immense gratitude goes to Dianne Morgan, John and Beverly Sanslow, Stuart and Debra Sedransky, John Weber, and many other people nationwide who read the book for correctness, suggestions, organization, meaningfulness, and theological soundness. They spent numerous hours carefully perusing the work and discussing topical issues with me.

Virginia Messer saw the publishing possibilities in my ideas and encouraged me to write this book. Her professionalism and expertise were invaluable on this project as she took it from manuscript to final product.

Melissa Roberts, as this work's editor, offered valuable insights and necessary critical analysis. Her perceptive observational skills have enhanced the quality of this project. Special thanks to this gifted professional.

I have received motivation for many years from watching my cousins and aunts overcome some of life's greatest challenges. Thanks to Charlotte and Mac Smith of Temple, Texas, and Gloria

Byrd McDonald and Ellna Pitts Byrd of Big Spring, Texas, for letting me tell their stories in this work. Posthumously, I offer gratitude to Frances Haydon Parnell of Arlington, Texas, and Nell Pitts Haydon of Temple, Texas, for inspiring me as I observed them courageously conquering their many life-battles against great odds. My appreciation to Charlotte Haydon Smith for granting permission to use the stories of her sister, Frances, and her mother, Nell.

As always, my husband, Ray Corbin, encourages me constantly. He is ceaselessly available as a sounding board for ideas and is patient with the grueling schedule that accompanies researching and writing a book. Ray is God's great gift to my life.

Thanks to all my friends and family who telephoned and e-mailed with words of encouragement, listened to my ideas and provided feedback, and enthusiastically saw the possibilities in this project.

Section 1

America's New Challenges

CHAPTER 1

Christian Responsibility

*"We cannot have relative values
in a nuclear world.
We will destroy one another."*

—Comment to author from a nuclear scientist

I had just finished my speech to a large delegation of nuclear science professionals gathered in Orlando, Florida. This meeting was held immediately before the UN weapons inspectors entered Iraq in the early fall of 2002 after a multi-year absence. One of the sponsors of this conference was the United Nations International Atomic Energy Agency (the international nuclear energy watchdog). As I left the stage and walked down the aisle, a conference participant stepped in front of me and said: "If the world becomes as you have just presented, the world cannot stand." I stopped to talk with him a few seconds concerning how American values are changing and our definitions of absolutes for right and wrong are blurring. He continued, "We cannot have relative values in a nuclear world. We will destroy one another." Defining moment! Realizing how fatal our weapons of mass destruction are and how many nations possess them, that conversation changed my life.

I have spent my twenty-five-year career speaking, training, and consulting with organizations of all types on how leaders can forecast the future and strategically plan for success. I have been blessed to work with some of the most prominent organizations in the world. From them, I have learned much. My career has been exciting and has taken me to places I could have only dreamed about as a child growing up on a farm in McKinney, thirty-two miles north of Dallas, Texas. However, I have always felt that as I helped organizations plan for the future, even as I authored books and articles about expectations of the future, there was something missing. I felt that I was not encouraging people to deal with the whole story. I sensed there was more to be said.

When that nuclear scientist made the comment about our dangerous world, I realized that I could no longer work in a vacuum. The whole story must be told. That story is this: No matter how humans plan and work for the future, we are not in ultimate control. God is. He can choose to make our plans happen or thwart them. He can choose to protect our nation or lift his hand of protection from us.

September 11, 2001

No involved American will ever forget the horrible day of September 11, 2001. It is one of those significant events that, when mentioned, people can tell you just where they were and what they were doing at the time. They will always be able to do that, just as I can definitely remember vivid details about my day on November 22, 1963, when President John F. Kennedy was assassinated. The events of September 11, 2001, now known as 9/11, gripped the nation. I remember watching as a second plane flew into the World Trade Center in New York City. Pictures of the Pentagon in flames flashed on TV. Rumors of a downed plane in Pennsylvania came on the air. I prayed: "God, please stop all this!"

Reflecting the perspective of Americans at the time, I did not know what was happening. Was there an invasion? Had a group of people gone mad? Was every major city going to be hit? How frightening! I was planning to fly out of Dallas-Fort Worth International Airport later on 9/11, but all flights were grounded before my plane could take off—even before I left my home for the airport. My telephones began to ring. Friends were calling my husband to inquire whether I was on one of the planes involved in the terrorist attacks. What a morning of pandemonium!

4

For months after that day of horror, talk show pundits, religious leaders, the news media, political scientists, and millions of Americans tried to make sense of what had happened. Deep philosophical and theological questions were debated on mainstream talk shows. Such questions as the following were asked: Did God cause 9/11? If He didn't, then why did He let it happen? Why did so many innocent people have to die? I, too, pondered those questions. However, not until my brief conversation with the nuclear professional did I see just what God might have been doing on 9/11.

I analyzed what God protected and on what God lifted his hand of protection. One theory is that the plane which hit the Pentagon was headed for the White House. Air traffic controllers were able to pick up the path. The trees around the White House had not yet lost their leaves on 9/11, so the hijacker, an inexperienced pilot, was unable to see the White House from the air. He turned and directed the plane into the Pentagon. The plane that crashed in Pennsylvania, after courageous passengers attacked the pilot/terrorist at the helm, was probably headed for the U.S. Capitol in Washington.

For some reason, God allowed the symbols of business, trade, finance, and power, as well as that of the military, to be attacked while protecting the symbols of the U.S. government. Why? Could it be a warning signal that we as Christians have begun to put our faith for safety and prosperity in material things and in our military might instead of in God? Could it be that God was giving our country another chance to remain supreme by protecting our government from all the social, political, and economic upheaval that surely would have followed? Is it possible that God was preparing America for a divine global destiny?

Still, though, my question of why so many good people died that day has not been answered. A minister I met in the airport shortly after 9/11 made a comment which helps me with that question. "Sometimes people," he told me, "are asked to pay a great price for God's kingdom. We must be willing." That's food for thought.

Although we realize that 9/11 was perpetrated by people determined to damage America, we also know from Romans 8:28 that God can take horrible events and use them for good outcomes for His people. Indeed He can use 9/11 as a warning signal for America. The lesson I received from analyzing events, and through much prayer, is that God is telling us that the symbols of business, money, and power as well as our military might have been the things in which we increasingly have placed our trust for thriving and surviving as a nation. In all our pride of accomplishment, we have forgotten the source of our security and protection—Almighty God.

America Changes Her Course

On March 19, 2003, the history of the United States intersected its future. A definite change took place as roles in the global power structure shifted. The mix of international alliances altered for the first time in several decades. Indeed, America assumed a new type of leadership position as she, along with an international coalition of willing nations, entered Iraq to remove the existing regime and release the Iraqi people from many years of oppression. Realizing that we live in a very dangerous world, the leaders of the United States, Great Britain, Spain, and Australia committed support and/or troops to begin the quest of making the world safe for democracy. The decision to conduct such activity was not popular in global opinion. These leaders were forced to choose between doing the popular thing and doing the right thing. They wagered their political futures on their decision. The "coalition of the willing," as these four nations along with many of their other allies have been labeled, chose to do the right thing.

Remembering the bloodbath that resulted from the tyranny of Adolf Hitler in the 1930s and 1940s during World War II, these leaders could not sit idly by and let similar tyranny cast its shadow on millions of innocent people. Sixty years after World War II, weapons of mass destruction are in the hands of evil rulers who intend to use them for destructive purposes. Biological, chemical, and nuclear weapons are deadly in the hands of corrupt despots. No person on earth is safe. These weapons have the potential to heap deadly destruction on all nations. The United States of America is determined to meet these global challenges head-on. We are living in very precarious times.

With terrorism and world events threatening America as never before, it is time for making obedience to God a priority. Only God can ultimately save our land. This is not to say that we should abandon all our financial and people resources along with our greatest, mightiest military in the world. That would not be logical or sensible. In fact, that choice would be suicidal. The idea is, however, that we must focus first and foremost on God and seek His direction for developing and using our other resources for keeping America free and its people safe from destruction. God demands priority status!

Where do we start? With God's people. The Bible, in 2 Chronicles 7:14, answers that question explicitly.

> If my people, which are called by my name, shall humble themselves, and pray, and seek my face, and turn from their wicked ways; then will I hear from heaven, and will forgive their sin, and will heal their land.

These were God's words to Solomon, king of Israel, after he had completed building the temple. In this verse, God proclaimed that if some sort of disaster struck the nation of Israel, He would save the Israelites if they would exercise specific behaviors. Through this conversation with Solomon, God provided four requirements of His people and three promises to His people, which continue to hold true today.

The majority of the remainder of this book will deal with these requirements and promises. But first, please note that moral greatness in America begins with God's people—not outside God's people. In the Old Testament, God's people were the Israelites. In the New Testament, God opens His invitation to become one of His people to all who sincerely put their ultimate faith in Jesus Christ by making Him Leader of their lives. Thus God's people today are obedient followers of Jesus Christ who have an intimate relationship with Him—Christians.

Many Christians look around themselves at the values of the world and are appalled at the moral decline over the past half-century. However, God tells us to look into the mirror at ourselves before looking outside Christianity. Every Christian has a specific role delegated by God for healing our land. Only through humility, prayer, seeking God's presence, and focusing on God's purpose (rather than our own selfish goals) will we find the part we are to play in the big picture—and the courage to step forward and assume our unique responsibilities. We are to execute the four requirements first before receiving God's promises for our nation. It is an awesome Christian responsibility to be standing in the gap between our nation's preservation and destruction.

Freedom is Earned

In working with myriad audiences throughout the past twenty-five years, prior to 9/11, I had become increasingly aware of the attitudes of many individuals that the freedoms we enjoy in the United States are rights to which we are entitled simply because we are Americans. When I heard such remarks, I would quickly point out that our freedoms have been purchased for an expensive price. Freedom is earned; it is never an entitlement. Each generation must do its part in assuring that America's freedom continues. I believe that the events of 9/11 and the new American role in meeting global challenges indicate that we, as Christians, must become involved in preserving America's future. It is a responsibility beginning with God's people and radiating to every citizen.

When a nation's morals weaken, the nation is vulnerable. God told Abraham in Genesis 15:13-16 that his people would inherit a promised land but not until 400 years later. By then, the sins of the Canaanites would be so great that God would allow them to lose their land, and the Israelites would be allowed to conquer them. Later, just before Joshua's war campaign, Moses told the people of Israel that God was allowing them to possess the land of Canaan, not because they were so righteous but because the Canaanites were so sinful (Deuteronomy 9:5). Rather than remaining pure and holy after conquering the Cannanites, the Israelites blended into the Canaanite culture of sexual misconduct and idol worship. God eventually allowed Israel to fall into Babylonian captivity because of moral decay.

Sodom and Gomorrah were destroyed, perhaps by volcanic eruption (Genesis 19:24-25), although scholars don't know for certain how they were obliterated. We read in Genesis 18 that Abraham bargained with God to preserve Sodom if he could find ten righteous men. That did not happen. Thus both cities of Sodom and Gomorrah were destroyed because of sexual promiscuity and violence, according to Biblical accounts. Additionally, in Ezekiel 16:49, Sodom is depicted as having been arrogant, wealthy, apa-

thetic, and insensitive to the poor and needy—factors which con
tributed to its demise.

Once the mightiest kingdom in the world, the ancient Roman
Empire eventually fell. Research indicates that the military weakened
because soldiers were no longer motivated to defend the nation
against invaders, the economy suffered, the infrastructure declined
into shambles, and Roman citizens lost their loyalty to the goals of
the once-great nation due to split allegiances to different religious
ideologies. Once strong, Rome became weak. (*The Fall of Rome*, retrieved April 1, 2003, from web site www.acs.ohio-state.edu/
history/isthmia/teg/Hist111H/issues/rome1.html)

Our Future Rests in God's Hands

History indicates that all great nations have eventually fallen.
The United States is the last remaining superpower. Our preemi-
nence in world affairs is not an entitlement. Our supremacy must
be preserved deliberately. Because our nation was founded on
Godly principles, the responsibility for the continued dominance of
this American way of life rests in the hands of God through His
people—Christians. What an awesome responsibility! However, in
order to renew America, Christians living in America must themselves experience renewal.

I am optimistic about the future of our great country. I believe
that America's best days lie ahead. I further believe that we will
overcome our challenges and work together to create a better world
for the generations that follow. My confidence lies in the fact that
God has provided a blueprint for our nation's greatness. I believe
that we have a divine global destiny.

Section 2

God's Requirements for Healing the United States of America

Chapter 2

Humble Yourself

It is tempting to give ourselves too much credit for our achievements in a wealthy and prosperous nation such as the United States.

The Twelve Step program of Alcoholics Anonymous has been adapted to many other processes for overcoming addictions. The first step in all these programs is to admit powerlessness over the dependency. Until we admit our need, we cannot receive help. This concept holds true for anything we want in life. Admitting that we are not in control and are in need of help is my definition of humility. We meet God at our point of need.

God values humility from His people. In Micah 6:8, we are told that the Lord requires us to walk humbly with God. Jesus said that humble people are blessed and inherit His kingdom (Matthew 5:3). The description Jesus gave of himself indicates that He was humble (Matthew 11:29). In order to heal our land, God requires humility. In fact, God requires humility to the point that He actively works against arrogant, proud people (James 4:6, Proverbs 3:34). He wants us to submit ourselves in obedience and to worship Him.

Americans are known as some of the most generous people in the world. In contrast, however, research shows that we live in a society that increasingly exhibits arrogance and rudeness. According to a study by Steve Farkas and Jean Johnson entitled *Aggravating Circumstances* and released by Public Agenda in 2002 (retrieved from Public Agenda web site, April 4, 2002, www.publicagenda.org), approximately 80 percent of the respondents say that rudeness is a problem and approximately 60 percent describe the problem as becoming progressively worse. Additionally, G. Loyd Rediger, in his book *Clergy Killers: Guidance for Pastors and Congregations under Attack* (Louisville, Kentucky: Westminster John Knox Press, 1997), the author feels that the church now reflects modern society to the point that one in four pastors have suffered abuse from congregational members.

Proverbs 16:19 instructs us that it is better to be humble and oppressed than to pillage with proud people. And the verse immediately before, Proverbs 16:18, indicates that destruction is the result of arrogant pride. In a competitive environment, it is difficult to be humble, especially when self-centered, strong, pushy people seem to zoom right past us on the way to the top. On work teams or volunteer committees, there is often a dominant, arrogant personality bent on controlling the group. I have noticed marriages wherein one spouse is verbally abusive and controlling of the other marital partner. The slate of arrogant people is long, and names of the humble comprise a rather short list.

Jesus demonstrated humility. After his birth, he was placed in an animal trough that served as his baby bed (Luke 2:7). As an adult, he lived in material poverty (2 Corinthians 8:9) and didn't even have a roof over his head. He declined human praise (John 5:41). His greatest act of humility was dying on the cross for the sins of the world (Hebrews 12:2). In His parable about seating at a wedding feast (Luke 14:7-11), Jesus warned against taking the best seat at the table in that the host might have to ask the guest to occupy a lesser seat if someone of higher status needed that seat. The first guest would then be embarrassed. He suggested taking the lesser seat in the first place. Jesus ended the parable by saying that humble people will be exalted and proud people will be humbled.

Adam and Eve got into trouble because of their pride. God set restrictions on their lives by requiring them to not avail themselves of the fruit of the tree of knowledge of good and evil in the Garden of Eden. However, they chose to disobey God and act independently—in spite of His warning (Genesis 3). They then caused all sorts of difficulty for themselves and all humankind thereafter. Down through the ages, it has been demonstrated that people get into deep trouble when they do not obey God. In fact, obedience is a confirmation of our love for God (John 14:15).

Exercising Humility

Someone once told me that a great way to practice humility is to always tell the truth. In today's competitive, prideful society, it's easy to stretch a point or exaggerate the importance of an action or achievement. Telling the truth is basic and a good first step to becoming humble. By studying the Bible thoroughly, you will find many scriptures dealing with humility. Worshipful obedience to God, the greatest act of human humility, requires that we know how to submit our egos and pride. A good place to start is with the Ten Commandments (Exodus 20:3-17) and then Jesus' summation of the two greatest commandments: to love God with the essence of your being and love others equal to yourself (Matthew 22:36-40). The Sermon on the Mount (Matthew 5-7) is very helpful for guidance in Christian living. All through the Bible, you will find helpful suggestions for remaining submissive to God and instructions for living a Godly life.

Can we abide by each command perfectly? No, because such behavior is impossible. That's why Christ died on the cross and rose again. His blood was a sacrifice in order that we would not be forced to live a faultless life in order to enter Heaven. His grace will take us there. The idea, however, is to continue to work with the Holy Spirit to become as much like Jesus Christ in character as possible on earth. We should never quit trying to improve. Jesus asks us to keep His commandments in sight at all times (John 14:15). In John 14:8-9, the scripture tells us that Jesus is God. Therefore, by emulating the character of Christ, we will please God and actually reflect the character of God Himself. The remainder of this chapter provides practical examples for exercising humility with other people.

Listening skills. When someone is speaking, it is helpful to concentrate on what the other person is saying. Devote full attention to the person who is talking. Often, people interrupt others before they are finished and continue with their own story. That shows lack of respect and is self-centered. Mostly the interruption occurs because someone wants to "top" the other person's story.

When a person is telling a story about how sick she has been, the other person can tell of a time when she was sicker. If someone is having problems with an aging parent, often he is interrupted by one who has had worse problems than that.

I have been guilty of interrupting from time to time. I remember the last time I did that. My friend's reply broke me of my bad habit. I don't even remember the story she was telling. However, after she finished, I began to tell about another situation that was equally bad or worse. My motive was sympathy and comfort. However, it evidently didn't sound that way to her. She waited until I finished and said: "OK, you win!" I stopped, looked at her questioningly, and seemed puzzled, I'm sure. She just laughed and went on to another subject. Later, when I began to think about what she meant, her words made sense. I had unknowingly tried to trump her story. From that moment on, I have always thought about how my words might be interpreted before I say them. I have also realized that most people just want you to listen and sympathize. They don't necessarily want to hear your story.

Willingness to serve. God sometimes asks us to serve in places and execute tasks that we consider boring or subservient. People who have important jobs in the workplace expect also to have important jobs in their community volunteer work or in their church tasks. Many of the assignments seem beneath them, in their view. However, God considers all people to be equal in His kingdom and considers no task too small. Jesus washed his disciples' feet, a very lowly task in that culture. If God can stoop to lowly activities, we should be willing to do the same.

My mother was a victim of Alzheimer's disease. She progressively declined mentally and then physically for eleven years. She was widowed twenty-three years before the onset of her disease and lived alone. I did not reside in her city. I wanted to keep her at home as long as possible because she had lived in her house all her married life. Old habits die hard. Thus even when her memory was lapsing, she, by habit, could continue to find things and live fairly well with assistance from nurses and other helpful people. She was blessed to be surrounded by the greatest Christian colleagues I have ever known. Most of these people were acquaintances who had experienced a full career and had retired. Some were bankers. Others were secretaries.

After their retirement, they chose to work on a part-time basis caring for the elderly. I watched as those women humbled themselves to execute tasks that were never required of them in their former working environment. Always smiling and enthusiastically changing beds, bathing my mother, and washing her clothing— among other such tasks as preparing meals and driving her to the hair salon—these people modeled Jesus to me. I have never had an experience quite like that. They were demonstrating Christian love to a family who desperately needed their help. They humbled themselves in service. I suspect that God was watching from Heaven and was very pleased. As the women provided Mother's care year after year, I often thought of Matthew 25:40, in which Jesus states that if you have done good things for His children, it's the same as having served Him.

Comparison to Jesus Christ. I once heard someone say: "Well, I'm certainly better than she is. Her language is deplorable. She's had an affair. And she is openly defiant of her husband in public. I don't do any of those things." By comparing ourselves to others, we can always find someone who has character flaws worse than ours, just as the above example illustrates. By choosing to compare ourselves to other people, we can manipulate our perceptions and look good to ourselves most of the time. That behavior is a combination of denial and rationalization.

God's idea is for us to compare ourselves to Christ. Immediately, that is a humbling experience. Jesus Christ was sinless. Humans commit sins by the minute. Jesus Christ was perfect. Humans are imperfect. Jesus Christ was obedient to God until death. Humans disobey God often.

Giving up control. The Serenity Prayer asks God to help the one who is praying to learn to let go of trying to control situations and people that he really has no control over. Perfectionists try to control all situations. They feel as if they have failed if they are not in control. Endeavoring to control everything is trying to play God. That is impossible. Even God offered freedom of choice to his created human beings. In so doing, He took the risk that humans would make wrong choices.

Letting go of control over people is a way to express love. Obviously, parents must maintain a certain amount of control over their children's behavior. However, even child-rearing experts suggest that choices be given to children whenever it would be wise to do so. The truest expression of love to others is through *agape*, which is God's love accessible only through a relationship with Jesus Christ. This highest order of love for others allows people the freedom to be themselves, choose their friends, prepare for a career, and pursue their God-inspired dreams. Letting go of control tells people they are important to you and that you have their best interest in mind. Only spiritually mature people are capable of practicing forms of *agape*.

Yielding your need to be right. Humble people choose their battles carefully. Those individuals with the need to be right all the time appear to be arrogant and uncaring. For example, Molly has studied hard all her life. Reading books and news media reports and absorbing political talk shows is a daily routine. She is a high-level intellectual who is impatient with people who are not as intellectually astute as she. Every time she hears someone utter a mispronounced word, Molly feels compelled to appoint herself to the "dictionary police" and correct the pronunciation. If a person misstates a fact, she is quick to question the data and goes into a long dissertation of why the person is wrong.

When Molly's friend, Alina, proudly tells her about a new car she just purchased, Molly quickly queries Alina on how much she paid, the terms and conditions of payment, and the degree to which she negotiated the deal. Of course, Molly emphasizes to Alina that she could have done better. Next time, Molly suggests, Alina should telephone her before going to the car dealership. Molly tells Alina she is certain she can help beat the deal on her next purchase. Molly is a perfectionist. Obviously, her arrogance is not popular among her few friends.

Some people need to be right to the extent that they can't face being wrong. They attempt to explain away any shortcomings or mistakes. By blaming other people for their blunders, they shift the responsibility for their own behavior to someone else. When people blame others for their deficiencies, they sacrifice the opportunity for spiritual growth.

Barry grew up in a family that worked hard. He had four brothers and sisters. Because his parents were always working to put food on the table, Barry felt that his parents didn't have time for him. He desperately sought their attention, but when they came home from work after eight to ten hours at the factory, they barely had time to have dinner, listen to the news, prepare clothes for the next day, then go to bed to get some rest for yet more hard work. Barry began to feel detached from his family. He questioned his importance. Desperately needing to belong somewhere, he joined a gang.

Before long, the gang's leaders were asking Barry to steal cars to prove his loyalty. Then they demanded that he join them in their drug activities. Barry's grades dropped. He was failing in school. Finally, he totally abandoned his educational pursuits. His parents were furious. They tried reasoning with him, threatening to take away his car, asking him to move out of the family's home—among many other idle threats. None of this communication worked. Barry eventually left home to live with one of his gang "brothers." They got into deeper trouble. Bank robbery charges were brought against Barry. He began serving a prison sentence.

When the youth minister of the local church heard about Barry's plight, he visited him in prison. Barry was bitter and claimed that his criminal behavior was all the fault of his parents. He hated all adults, he told the minister. The rules of society are stupid, he believed. He had the attitude that it was "Barry against everybody else." The youth minister left feeling that only the Holy Spirit could reach Barry. He put him on the church's prayer list and planned to visit him regularly in prison in order to try to gain Barry's trust.

Because of his ever-present need to be right, Barry could never accept responsibility for his behavior. Even the consequences of his crimes were harsh, he felt. He was desperately angry at law enforcement officers. He could not face the fact that he was responsible for his own actions—and therefore had to face the consequences.

Highly competitive people also have the need to be right. Their motive in life is to trump the competition. They view life as a win-lose situation. Even when they are participating in a casual sport, it isn't long before they begin to take the game seriously. They play to win every time. Often people affected by this attitude have their self-esteem tied to external events. They feel good about themselves only when they are winning. When they lose, as they sometimes will, they become totally depressed. Their moods rise and fall with life events. They are hollow internally. Either people never learned or have forgotten that self-esteem is generated by the Holy Spirit in relation to God's purpose for their lives. Self-worth lies in pursuing a God-given purpose. When people believe that, they can overcome any obstacle because their self-worth doesn't bobble, and their stress level is greatly reduced.

Humble people have great courage. When they are wrong, they are strong enough to apologize. I have an elderly friend who told me that in her seventy-year marriage, her husband has never said "I love you" or "I'm sorry." What a lonely, strained life this couple must have lived. How sad that they have never known the verbal intimacy that these two statements can generate.

Showing empathy. Humility puts other people first. Humble people realize that life is not about them. It's about serving God and other people without neglecting their own personal needs to the point of self-abuse. Empathy causes you to mentally project yourself into another person's situation and try to understand their predicament. It is helpful to find out their background, understand their culture, and grasp their philosophy of life.

Nianna befriended Jackson, who had been divorced twice, when they were both doing volunteer work at an inner city school. They found that they had much in common and began to have dinner together occasionally. Nianna sensed that Jackson was emotionally needy in several ways. Her nurturing personality caused her to try to help Jackson with some of his problems. She had to be cautious not to enable Jackson to become needier. She had to carefully balance empathy and enablement. Nianna wanted to understand Jackson and try to help him without causing him to become dependent on her and again deny his role in taking responsibility for his divorces.

Nianna soon noticed that Jackson did most of the talking. She did most of the listening. The conversation was all about him. He desperately needed someone who would listen to him and provide encouragement. Jackson expected Nianna to be available to him but never seemed to be available when Nianna needed him. Their friendship became one-way. Nianna was mature enough as a Christian to understand that some friendships are that way and that God sometimes assigns us to needy people to help them face the truth in themselves. Nianna recognized that God wanted her to help Jackson. In order to do that, Nianna made certain that her needs were met by God through other people and that she did not depend on Jackson for anything. She was there to give—not to get. Her job was that of encouragement.

Nianna asked probing questions about Jackson's background. She understood his family culture. His emotional outbursts, she decided, reflected his years of abuse as a child. She learned not to take his anger personally but as a cry for help. Nianna asked God for strength to support her through this friendship. Most people would have either gotten too involved with Jackson and thereby suffered hurt or abandoned him altogether, because friendships like this are hard. Nianna, however, believed beyond the shadow of a doubt that God had placed her in Jackson's life. She was determined to stay the course and remain spiritually healthy throughout her God-given assignment.

Today, almost twenty years later, Jackson is an emotionally healthy man who is serving his community and church, has a very responsible career position in a major nonprofit agency, and is a model husband and father of four wonderful children. Jackson progressed to the person he has become today partly because Nianna realized that life is not always about her and dared to exercise empathy with another person.

Reducing attachment to material possessions. I read an editorial written in response to the events of 9/11 in a major secular periodical. I don't remember where I read it; however, it warned Americans to be careful of attaching themselves tightly to this world because this world will eventually break their hearts. That concept is not new. My surprise came in discovering the statement in a secular magazine. Jesus told us that we cannot serve God and material things (Matthew 6:24). We must choose our priority.

I am now involved in an exciting project that is aimed at creating a school capable of preparing learners to live and work in the future. First, our "think tank" painted a picture of the future as we saw it; then we determined the skills and processes a person must possess in order to live and work in such an environment. That was a daunting task. Tomorrow will not be like today. Tomorrow's problems must be solved with tomorrow's solutions. One discussion in the think tank concerned how we can train people to build their self-esteem on something other than personal accomplishments, acquisition of money and power, and winning in competition. In the world of the not-too-distant future, rapid change and global instability will cause people to be "on top" in a work environment and later be unemployed. When people are working, they feel empowered; when they are unemployed for a few months, they label themselves internally as losers. Depression sets in. The question in the think tank became: How can we teach young people that their self-esteem is not dependent on whether they win or lose in the material world? The only true answer to that is found in our faith. Without God purposing our life, and our discovering that life-purpose, we are hopelessly lost in a foggy sea of confusion and self-deception.

Humility dictates that we don't need ostentation in order to feel good about ourselves. Who we are is not about our earthly things. It's about Whose we are for eternity. That concept is becoming increasingly harder for Christians to grasp as our attitudes and emotional needs reflect contemporary culture.

Recognizing the need to worship with God's people. Humility also means determining that we cannot serve God in isolation nor can we live a Christian life without the support of fellow believers who will help hold us accountable for our life choices and behaviors. The author of Hebrews recognized that Christians need to be boosted by other Christians when he urged the early Jewish converts to Christianity to continue meeting together and encouraging one another (Hebrews 10:25).

It's no different today. The best place to find support of other Christians is in your local church. The percentage of regular church attendees has declined over the past fifty years. Depending on the city and state surveyed, church attendance in any one week varies from 10 percent to 45 percent of the population. Yet, according to a City University of New York study, 77 percent of Americans claim to be Christians. (Barry A. Kosmin, Egon Mayer, and Ariela Keysar, *American Religious Identification Survey,* 2001, The Graduate Center of the City University of New York) For a number of reasons, Christians have quit going to church regularly, if at all. I have heard all sorts of excuses for dropping out of church:

- The church is not relevant to my needs.
- I work all week and need to rest on Sunday mornings.
- I learned all that as a child and don't need to review the material again.
- Church bores me.
- I don't like the way people act in church. They are no better than the people at work.

• I can worship out in nature, on the golf course, or by listening to sermons on television just as well as I can by attending church.

Of course, there are even more excuses I haven't mentioned. However, each of these excuses can be countered. If you feel that the church is not relevant, then start attending so that you can be a positive force in changing the church. Most people are not acquainted with Biblical teachings. Their concept of God derives from TV talk shows, other religions, and conversations with friends. They did not master Biblical teachings as a child. Some churches are not boring. Find one that has exciting people and creative activities. Sunday is not the only day to attend church services. Bible study groups, small sessions, and worship services can be found at some churches throughout the week. All people in the church are sinners. Nobody is perfect. Hopefully, people are there with the motive of refining their character in order to reflect the character of Jesus Christ. Church is designed to be a place of worship and support—not an entertainment facility. We are God's people, not entertainment critics.

For several years after I finished college, I did not attend church regularly. I gave all the above excuses—and more. I visited church after church. I couldn't find one that interested me or one in which I felt I wanted to serve Christ. Further, I felt that I could worship God well in front of the television or at our farm where I could sense nature—God's creation. Friends would gather in our home, and discussion would sometimes lead to commentary on God's character. We felt certain we knew Him well.

Finally, the Holy Spirit tugged at me until I realized that I was wrong. I needed to be in church. I needed to worship God in church as well as any other place I chose. Worship can take place daily no matter where you are. But that does not preclude worship with fellow believers.

My husband and I set a goal of becoming active in church. After that deliberate decision, something amazing happened. When we discovered that it was our responsibility to *serve* a church rather than *to be served by* a church, we found the right place. I have learned more about the Bible and Jesus' teachings in the last fifteen years than I learned in my total life up to that point, including the twenty years I was in regular attendance in childhood, teen years, and in college. I found that I knew nothing compared to what I now know. And I don't know nearly as much now as I must know in the future to fully understand God's will for my life. The idea is to practice lifelong spiritual growth. That only happens when you are serving in a loving church while creating community with fellow supportive believers.

God Requires Humility

For God to heal our land, He requires humility of His people. It isn't an option (Micah 6:8). The opposite of humility is arrogance, and God specifically takes action against people who are prideful (James 4:6). When we are conceited, we are acting as if we ourselves are gods. We are usurping the prerogative of our Creator God. It is tempting to give ourselves too much credit for our achievements in a wealthy and prosperous nation such as the United States. However, we will always be humbled when we remember that God is in ultimate control. Our power is small compared to His. Our accomplishments are impossible without His guidance and grace. We are incapable of lasting success without His providential hand protecting our future.

CHAPTER 3
Pray

*Christianity is a relationship
with Jesus Christ,
not a religion demanding
observance of legal rules.*

Christianity is a relationship with Jesus Christ, not a religion demanding observance of legal rules. It is a relationship emanating from love and gratitude. Relationships cannot grow without communication. It is impossible to know another person well without dialoguing to discover her thoughts, values, dreams, and deepest beliefs. The same holds true for God. We cannot know God well unless we engage in conversation with Him. And God requires prayer from His people in order to heal our land.

Prayer is that conversation necessary for intimacy with God. As communication experts teach, effective communication must be two-way. One person talks; the other listens. Then the roles reverse. Throughout the dialogue, roles of talker and listener intermittently reverse and play out. Dialogue moves between sender and receiver just as a tennis ball moves between two players on the court.

If I were to ask you the name of a song that is playing right now on your favorite radio station (assuming you don't have your radio on), you probably couldn't tell me. There would be no way to know unless you were tuned to the correct radio frequency. Similarly, until you actively tune into God, you will never know Him. You won't know what He wants to reveal to you until you "tune in" through prayer. In Jeremiah 33:3, the Lord gives instruction to call on Him. He promises to answer and reveal things you did not know before you prayed.

It has become a habit of many people to go to God in prayer only in their desperation. When they are in their deepest state of panic, they turn to God. For the remainder of the time, they hardly think about Him, much less hold regular conversations with Him. In the hustle and bustle of life, it's easy to get into the daily grind and not take time for God. When a tragedy occurs, we then cry out for help. We meet Him at our point of need. And God hears our prayers. Moses told the Israelites that God's people would find God if they would search for Him with all their hearts and souls. (Deuteronomy 4:29)

When the United States was involved in the Persian Gulf War in 1991, Americans held prayer sessions. Churches opened their doors to special prayer gatherings. The same happened after 9/11. Each time, there was hope that America had experienced a spiritual awakening. However, after fear and intensity resulting from the events waned, people quit gathering for group prayers in the great numbers that had turned out during each crisis. I have heard pastors say that returning to "normal" after each incident had good and bad news attached. The good news is that people felt relatively safe again. The bad news is that people gathered in prayer less when the crises passed. Once again we are having special prayer sessions now that troops are committed to the 2003 Iraqi liberation operation and perhaps prolonged global tensions on other fronts. Hopefully, this time, individual and group prayers for our nation will continue with regularity and intensity. The United States is meeting its greatest challenges since World War II.

To truly walk with God, there must be constant communication by telling God how grateful you are for your blessings, asking Him to direct your life-path, seeking wisdom for decisions, petitioning for physical and emotional needs, and asking God to help other specific people you name—among many other requests and expressions of thankfulness. After you speak to God, listen. Spend quiet time listening to His conversation with you. Listen to what He says back to you through the Holy Spirit. He may cause a thought to surface or a helpful Bible verse to come to mind. He might direct you to seek out special people or guide you in taking specific actions. The human brain is the central control center for communication with God. He talks to you through your thoughts. The Spirit of Holiness, or Holy Spirit as He is known, speaks directly to you nonverbally. After you have prayed, in God's time, seemingly coincidental or accidental events may occur. Those could be God's answers to your prayers. When you are totally tuned into and focused on God, nothing is an accident. He can take any happening in your life and weave it into His purpose for you. To monitor your life's direction, however, you must stay in constant contact with God.

I recall one incident in which I had come to the end of my abilities for making good decisions about my mother, who was suffering from Alzheimer's disease. At one point, she had not yet quit driving her automobile. She had lost her way one night while driving home from the grocery store. A stranger had found her and guided her home. Mother didn't know her and couldn't remember her name. I never found out who she was. She must have been an "angel unawares" (see Hebrews 13:2). My mother telephoned me to tell me what had happened. I felt totally devastated. The moment had arrived that I had always dreaded—taking her car keys and discussing with her why she would be unable to drive her car anymore. I drove from Dallas the next morning and transported her to the hairdresser's salon. After I dropped her off, I went to the local restaurant for a cup of coffee while waiting to return to the hair salon to pick her up. Sitting in the booth alone with my back to other people in the restaurant and gazing out the window into the lovely morning sunlight, I prayed to God for answers. How would I break the news to her? How could I provide transportation on a regular basis since I did not live in the same city and was out of town almost all week every week? The city had no cab service.

I launched so deeply into prayer that I was totally unaware of my surroundings for ten or fifteen minutes. Then the answer came to me. It's as if God had directly spoken—and He had. He told me to get up from the table at that moment and go to the organization where Mother's neighbor worked part-time and ask if she would help with Mother's transportation needs for a monthly retainer. I had met the neighbor only once. She and her husband were new to

27

the neighborhood. Upon approaching her and her husband, they both readily agreed to help. They were both retired and were happy to have the extra income. One of their duties was to take Mother to church each Sunday and to her Golden Age group through the week. They told me that my proposal was an answer to their prayers in that they had been praying for a church to attend. That solved their dilemma. How wonderfully God works things out when we humbly turn to Him. He answered two prayers that day— mine and theirs.

Some scientific studies identify a "God spot" in the brain, an area hard-wired for God. (Vince Rause, "Searching for the Divine," *Reader's Digest,* December 2001) In that area of the brain, there is detected activity when one is praying or connecting with God. I like to use the analogy of the electric wall socket and the lamp plug. Electricity in the wall socket is there waiting to provide light if we only plug in the wire to the lamp. God operates the same way. He waits to light our path. However, it is our responsibility to plug into Him for direction.

Qualities of Prayer

To explore major qualities of prayer, it is important to research some of the prayers of Jesus Christ. By examining His prayers, we find examples of conversations with God that are essentially set forth by God Himself.

Highest expression of human spirituality. In Matthew 11: 25-26, Jesus expresses humility and thanksgiving as He opens His conversation with God. He tells God that He realizes that the wise, prudent, and educated people who don't know Him do not have the privilege of knowing what God reveals to His people. Jesus connects with his Father in an intimate way that humans who do not know the truth about God will never be able to do. Connection with God in conversation is spiritual, not physical. When we talk with God, we are communicating with eternity at the highest level of spirituality. We lose the presence of time and space while we are suspended in the face of God.

Jesus further indicates that prayer is one-on-one with God, and not for ostentation. Many people hope that great numbers of people will recognize their ability to articulate an extensive vocabulary

28

and thus provide long, beautiful speeches instead of sincere prayers. Jesus warns against this public display in Matthew 6:5-8. In this verse, however, He is not precluding public prayer nor prayer within a group of people. His concern is that people will pray with the wrong motive.

Display of humility. Jesus prayed in a garden of olive trees called Gethsemane just before he was betrayed by Judas and then arrested (Matthew 26:36-44). In fact, he prayed three times. Each time, he asked God to "take this cup from me." The "cup" represented the total of the world's sins which He would absorb with His blood that would be shed later on the cross in order to seal God's New Covenant (New Testament) with humanity. However, each time he petitioned, he also told God that He would abide by His will, not that of His own. In order that the scriptures could be fulfilled, Jesus Christ was destined to die on the cross for the sins of the world.

Evidence of trust. Just before Jesus' final prayer on the cross, supernatural events happened. Darkness reigned for three hours. Historical records from other countries actually show that about that time of day in that year, during the three hours of darkness, all the earth stood still. When the records of other countries were recorded, they knew nothing about the death of Jesus.

At the moment of Jesus' death, the earth shook. The curtain dividing the Holy of Holies from the more public place in the temple was torn into two pieces. The Holy of Holies was the sanctuary of God. Only the high priest could enter it; and he entered only once per year. The tearing of the curtain signifies our ability to go directly to God after Jesus' death without going through the high priest. Jesus is now our high priest. (Hebrews 9:1-15)

Jesus was indeed the Son of God. The second part of the Holy Trinity. The true revelation of our Creator. The Savior of all humankind. He had innocently died for all humankind as the scriptures had predicted. He was innocent yet was crucified as guilty. As He was dying, He prayed to God that He was committing His spirit to Him. (Luke 23:46) Jesus trusted God to the point of death—and into all eternity.

Private and/or public. After a day of bad news about the beheading of John the Baptist (His cousin), healing the sick and lame, and feeding 5,000 people, Jesus wanted solitary time with God.

29

With an eventful day like that, He deserved some quiet moments! He retired to a mountainside to pray and seek solace with God. (Matthew 14:12-23) In silence, we are at our best in conversation with God. In serenity, we can hear God's response to us.

Jesus also advocated public prayer if your motives are on the right track. In Matthew 18:19, Jesus indicates that if two people agree upon something to ask God for, it will be granted, assuming, of course, that it's within God's will that the people have petitioned. Thus we have an example of public prayer—prayers among people.

On behalf of others. While hanging on the cross, Jesus prayed that those who crucified Him would be forgiven. (Luke 23:34) His lips were parched. His body was pierced with spike-like nails. He had been offered wine mixed with gall to drink. The soldiers mocked Him. Yet, in all that defamation and pain, Jesus asked God to forgive those who had done that to Him. Jesus told God that the people did not recognize the severity of their sin. They evidently had no clue that He was God.

What a message for us today! In a time when corporate executives, through wrongdoing, are leaving thousands of employees stranded and jobless with little or no retirement funds after many years of company loyalty, it is easy to be bitter. When terrorism is striking our soil and terrorists are killing innocent people around the world, it is easy to hate. When the media reports that church leaders are exhibiting immoral character, it is easy to be cynical. But, in all this, Jesus asks us to follow His lead and forgive them. In one of Jesus' prayers known as the Lord's Prayer, which is to be a model prayer for all Christians, Jesus asks God to forgive the sins of people on the basis of how they forgive those who treat them wrongly. (Matthew 6:12,14-15) In the days when Jesus offered these prayers, it was unheard of to forgive someone who had committed a wrong. People were vindictive. In the Roman empire, when a property owner was murdered, all the slaves were put to death without question—just in case one of them committed the crime. Life was cheap. What a horrible existence. People had little mercy on others. It is important, however, to note that forgiveness does not excuse people from legal consequences of their wrongs against humanity.

In John 17:6-19, Jesus prayed for his disciples. He prayed for their protection in the world and for their unity with God. Further, in John 17:20-26, Jesus extended His prayer for all those who believe in Him to be protected in the world and to be one with God. In these prayers, Jesus turned over his earthly mission to those who believe in Him and asked God to protect them as they do God's will. As Jesus prayed for His followers, we are to pray for other believers. Jesus recognized that living in a world apart from Heaven would be difficult. There will be temptations, hurts, sicknesses, accidents, pain, criticism, mistreatment, punishment, and grief. Yet Christians are to persevere in this environment. Jesus expected us to pray for each other so that God can provide strength for the journey and believers can carry out their life-purpose.

Additionally, Christians are to pray for non-believers. We are to pray that they will discover their isolation from God and experience a personal life-transformation that only belief in God and obedience to Him can bring. I believe that we are to pray for the perpetrators of evil in the world that they will discover the real life through Jesus Christ, which offers love and grace, rather than the life they are living, which offers anger and hate. We must pray for our nation's positive future. We must pray that Christians will turn to God for their needs, take time to be with Him, and take inventory of their lives to see if they are behaving as Jesus Christ exemplified through His character. Then we are to pray for individual needs of others specifically. We must pray that their needs will be met. Prayers of intercession (on behalf of others) and interception (to change the course of events) can change the world. And today, America needs nation-changing prayers from God's people.

Important. Believers are expected to pray. Conversation with God is a "given." In the Lord's Prayer, Jesus said "when you pray" and provided an example. He didn't say "if you talk with God." He didn't say "when conditions are right, you might want to connect to your Creator." What He said was "when you pray," assuming that all believers will pray to their God. (Luke 11:2)

Jesus knew that we couldn't have a relationship with God without prayer. We can't know God without direct communication. We can't know God without talking and listening to His responses for life-guidance and wisdom. In the model prayer, Christ asks us to revere God, and open our prayers with a statement of thanksgiving and reverence. Then He asks for God's kingdom to come to earth.

And we need to pray for God's kingdom here on earth, the universal church, which unites the souls of all believers living and dead. The church is more than a physical location or building. It is a union of believers' souls in a spiritual sense. We ask Him to do His will on earth in our lives. Asking for material needs to be met, we can expect our prayers to be answered and we will want for nothing. Thus we need not worry about anything. (Matthew 6:25-32)

We are to ask God to forgive our sins to the degree that we forgive other people who sin against us. That's difficult to do, but when we do, it makes our lives better. Additionally, we are to ask God to keep us from temptation. It also helps if we stay away from temptations we know about. Then we petition to be delivered from evil that surrounds us. Finally, we are to recognize God's power to move Heaven and earth and know that He is eternal (beyond space and time). We end with Amen (meaning "so let it be, God"). Luke's version of the Lord's Prayer is shorter than Matthew's. For more verbiage and a complete version, see Matthew 6:9-13.

Hints for a Successful Prayer Life

For many years I managed to work God in over a quick cup of coffee or while driving in heavy traffic with the radio blaring loudly. It seemed that God received my non-quality time. One day I realized how much I valued time with my close friends. I made special efforts regularly to clear my calendar to be with them either in person or via telephone. In between those times, we would often e-mail a short message. I compared my desire to make time for friends with the quality of time I was giving to God, my greatest Friend. I was appalled that I was putting my dialogue with God under the heading of "when I get around to it." My time with Him obviously wasn't a priority in my daily schedule. When I noticed my mistake, I quickly rearranged my schedule so that I could offer God quality time each day. That rescheduling of activities refreshed my life.

Your prayer life can be orchestrated for highest quality. When your connection to God is in good condition, the rest of your life is better. Your attitude is positive. Problems are solved more easily. Your day goes more smoothly. Here are some hints for increasing the quality of your prayer life.

Block off time for God. It is helpful to give God thirty minutes to one hour of your undivided attention per day. It will make a tremendous difference in your life. Many people have a source of devotionals they read. Then they spend time meditating on the thoughts in the devotional and on the scriptures attached to the theme of the day. It's amazing how much you will learn from God by listening to His guidance for an uninterrupted period of time.

When I have expressed this idea to some of my professional colleagues, they look at me strangely and ask if I have any idea of their frenzied schedules. They tell me they don't even have time to soak in the Jacuzzi, much less carve out a half hour for prayer and meditation. We then delve into discussion concerning their schedules and priorities. Perhaps it would be helpful if they would take stock of their lives and reestablish their priorities. It is true that we always have time for those things we put first. Whatever a person doesn't have time for is not a priority at that moment in life. Time is a great asset. We spend it, or waste it, according to our discretion. It amazes me that people are looking forward to spending eternity with God and can't find a few minutes per day to get to know Him in this life. Eternity exists now. When you are submitted to the will of God, you will experience Heaven on earth—although you can't experience Heaven's fullness until you actually abide there after physical death.

King David must have set aside time in his mornings to pray. In Psalm 5:3, David indicates that God hears his prayers in the morning—the time when he petitions and expects answers. David was the first good king of Israel. Though he wasn't perfect, he had constant connection to God. He strayed from God's ways, but always came back to God in obedience.

Grow close to God. Seek spiritual union with Him. James, brother of Jesus and leader of the Jerusalem church, tells us to draw close to God, and He will draw close to us. (James 4:8) The suggestion in this verse is that if we are to be close to God, it will be up to us. If we grow distant from God, He seems unavailable and far away. If we make an effort to remain intimate with God, we will perceive Him as being available. The choice is ours. God is constant. He does not change. He doesn't come into our lives and then abandon us. Once we let Him into our lives, He remains forever. We determine the degree of intimacy we have with our Savior.

There is no greater intimacy than the true expression of love.

We love God because He loved us first (1 John 4:19). A close friend of Jesus who chose to stay in the area of the Savior's tomb and not abandon Him after the crucifixion, the apostle John, knew the deep love of friendship. In his letter (1 John 4:16), the apostle further tells us that "God is love." God is the essence of love, of everything in the world that is loving. And love heals. As we become more lovable, God seems more loving.

All the global conflict we are experiencing is a result of hate, anger, bitterness, miscommunications, and evil motives. It is impossible to enumerate all the energy and money being spent on trying to control the spread of evil and danger in the world. How much more productive we would all be if we could cooperate in a bond of love with unity toward a common goal for humankind. Love is a positive motivator. Hate kills people, dreams, economies, and world powers. When God's people turn back to Him, we must seek intimacy with Him. We must turn to Him in a spirit of love. By being close to Him, we can sense His presence. He can then help us do our part in healing the world.

Practice authenticity. God can see right through our pretenses. He knows us more intimately than anyone else. After all, we are His creation. My friend's son lost his job recently. I noted to her that he seemed calm about the whole situation. "When I had lunch with him yesterday," I commented to her, "he seemed as if he were enjoying the time off and looking forward to getting some rest from his harried schedule before going forward on his job hunt."

"I don't think so," she replied. "Although he tries to be 'up' when he talks to me, I can tell by the tone of his voice that he is really worried. The high-tech sector has been hit especially hard, and competition is fierce for jobs in that marketplace. I know him. He's my son. I sense when he's covering his feelings." If a mother knows her son well, and most moms do, then God knows us even better. He knows our weaknesses and strengths. He can see right through our excuses. He discerns whether we are facing the truth about ourselves. God is a reality God—not a God of pretense and falsehoods. We cannot deceive God. In fact, we can deceive ourselves more easily that we can deceive God.

When we dialogue with God, he wants us to be real. He values our authenticity. Often in my intimate times with Him, I have faced some shortcomings in myself that I had been disguising for years.

God wants to help and heal, not to scold and condemn. The mission of Christ in this world is found in John 3:17—to heal (or save) the world. It's that simple. And His people should be on a mission to heal the world.

In dialogue with God, verbalization is helpful. However, God can read our thoughts. It is possible to talk with God without overt verbalization. Technology experts tell us that we will be able to insert chips into our brains and read one another's thoughts within the next twenty-five years. Frankly speaking, that's not inviting to me or to many other people. I don't want folks to be able to read some of my thoughts. However, if computer scientists and engineers can develop tools to read thoughts, then we know God has had that capability at his disposal since creation. After all, science discovers, records, and makes new combinations and derivations from what God has already created.

Be specific, if possible. It is helpful to be specific in our conversations with God. However, when we just cannot seem to get our thoughts together, the Holy Spirit can petition and express our thoughts for us. Sometimes we reach the end of ourselves and cannot express our prayers to God. If that becomes the case, merely set aside your time with God, do the best you can, then listen to what God tells you. The Holy Spirit will intervene on your behalf. (Romans 8:26-27)

Specificity creates clarity in our own minds. When we know exactly what we are petitioning God to do, or for whom we are asking intercessions, or in what event we are asking God to intervene, we can hold lucid conversations with God and are better prepared to find direction in what He tells us. In other words, we are more focused. Thus, it is important to make a special effort to approach God with specifics. But that procedure isn't required. God can help us in spite of our lack of clarity.

Approach God positively. Mark indicated, through the words of Jesus, that we are to expect to receive what we ask for in prayer (assuming it is in the realm of God's will). In the book of Mark, verse 24 of Chapter 11, Jesus asks His followers to assume that they have already received what they have asked for in prayer. You can't get more positive than that! One of the laws present throughout the Bible is that of sowing and reaping. In other words, we reap what we sow. If we plant wheat seeds, a crop of wheat will grow—

35

not corn or some type of fruit. In the same sense, if we plant positive thoughts in prayer, positive results happen. Even when Jesus was agonizing in Gethsemane, He was positive and submitted. He ended His three prayers committed to God's will and in positive acceptance of the outcome prophesied in the Old Testament.

In the Lord's Prayer, Christ's statements are positive and expectant. It is obvious that He expects God to give Him what He is asking for. Positive prayers are affirming to the one who prays and also to God.

Listen. When we are quiet and still, we can hear and experience God (Psalm 46:10). God whispers in the quiet moments with our Savior. His still voice speaks in tones audible only to those who know Him (John 10:4).

I have also found that when I have made a specific request to God, He may answer me at a time when I least expect. It's as if an invisible antenna for God's answers raises when I ask God for something. Later, when I am reading the Bible, a specific verse may take on a different meaning than ever before and help me with a dilemma. Or I may be having a conversation with a friend, and my answer happens from that verbal interchange. Often a specific verse from the Bible pops into my thoughts and provides direction. That's why it is so important to study the Bible. The Holy Spirit uses that text as one way to talk with us.

One of my most remarkable answers to prayer came at the nuclear science conference in Orlando that I mentioned at the beginning of Chapter 1. I had been sensing for more than seven years that God was pointing me toward coupling my present career with spirituality and even pursuing doctoral work at a theological seminary. Yet I felt no real direction. The tugging was there, but the path was not definite—not even the first step. I took the course by Dr. Henry Blackaby entitled "Experiencing God" (Nashville, Tennessee: LifeWay Press, 1990). From that course, I diagnosed that I was indeed experiencing God. But what did God want? Why was I so confused? Why were there so many unanswered questions? Throughout the program, Dr. Blackaby told us, as participants, to keep doing what we were doing until God answered.

I am not the most patient person in the world, but I chose to follow Dr. Blackaby's advice. I kept on doing what I was doing. My career continued to develop and take me down interesting paths. I even wrote another book during that time. And it was when the nuclear professionals discovered that book, *Great Leaders See the Future First,* and asked me to speak on it at their Orlando conference, that my answer came.

After seven years of internal questioning and prayer, the nuclear profesional stepped out into the aisle and made the statement I related to you in Chapter 1 concerning the dangerous state the world is now experiencing. Immediately, God's answer hit me. I knew beyond a shadow of a doubt what God expected of me. I came home, began searching for a seminary, and found the ideal one that could work with my travel schedule. What's more, the seminary had a doctoral concentration in conflict management. That's the issue I wanted to study. In a research project I had conducted for Leadership USA in 1998, I had identified five major global conflicts: one was religious conflict motivated by religious fundamentalists and the need for positive resolution. If not resolved, we had forecast that the world would catapult into social and economic chaos. My antenna was up. The lengthy search had culminated in positive results.

My twenty-five-year career had been preparing me for that decision. God had waited until world events intersected my preparation. Now I realize God's purpose. He knew all these conditions would occur in the global arena and made certain I was prepared through experiences before revealing His plans. He designed His timing for this moment. He is constantly whispering. It is important for all Christians to listen for Him and avoid letting the noise and clatter of the world's lesser priorities drown Him out.

Meditate. Some religions other than Christianity emphasize meditation. As a result, many Christians feel that meditation is wrong and ineffective. However, meditation is stipulated of God's people in the Bible as Paul requested of Timothy in 1 Timothy 4:15. Paul is writing to Timothy and providing instructions for spiritual growth and development. He asks Timothy to meditate on the things he is telling him.

Meditation involves selecting a subject or a Bible verse and thinking about it deeply. It's the same principle we use when we worry—except meditation is positive. The way Christian meditation differs from meditation of other religions is that other religions require followers to empty their minds and disconnect from all attachments. In Christian meditation, we are asked to connect to something specific. Paul, in Philippians 4:8, asks Christians to think about positive, true, and wonderful things. King David asks God to let his thoughts (meditations) be pure in His sight in Psalms 19:14. Thus Christian meditation is a tool that causes us to grow spiritually. God speaks to us through our meditations. Prayer life is not complete without setting aside time to think on the things of God.

Chapter 4
Seek God's Presence

When you feel that inner tugging
(the Holy Spirit)
urging you to do something, do it.
Trust your God-instincts.

My favorite time of the day is sunrise. When the sun peeks over the eastern horizon and displays the crisp dawn, it seems as if God is proclaiming the chance to begin again. I often stroll in my backyard gardens sensing the freshness of a new day. The birds warble hopeful trills. The freshness of the dew on the flowers inspires my senses. And the presence of God is overwhelming. In the stillness, I sense God's breath—His omnipresent Spirit.

The psalmist proclaimed: "... my heart and my flesh crieth out for the living God." (Psalm 84:2) The very center of his being and his whole body longed for God. The psalmist is seeking God's face—a term often used in the Old Testament to mean that someone is looking for God's presence—trying to find God's Spirit. According to God's instructions to Solomon for healing the land, God's people are to seek His face. We are to pursue His presence. God's Spirit lives in Christians. God's presence is continually with us—although sometimes God seems closer than at other times. Jesus told his disciples that the Holy Spirit would come and dwell within them in order that they could continue to learn and move toward spiritual maturity. (John 14:26) That same God-Spirit dwells within all believers.

Our God is with us all the time. When I sense His presence in my gardens, that's because I'm meditating on the wonders of His creation. When I sense him in illness or danger, that's because I'm seeking Him at my point of need. In other words, when we focus on God's presence, we will see His face. The key word here is *focus*. Peter, when walking out from his fishing boat to meet Jesus in the water, lost his focus on Jesus because a wind came up and frightened Peter. He quit looking at Jesus and started concentrating on his fear, which overcame his faith and confidence. As a result, Peter began to sink. In desperation he screamed to Jesus to save him. Jesus reached out His hand. Peter took it. And Jesus helped him climb back into the boat. (Matthew 14:28-31)

That story has been a favorite of mine since childhood. It so vividly illustrates what happens when we take our focus off God. We begin to sink. Not everyone reaches out his hand for Jesus as did Peter. Many people try to save themselves. They reach for an illusive life raft, which may come in the form of drugs (of which alcohol is most abused), putting their hopes in other people, or an escape into pornography. The quest for survival might appear in the form of an eating disorder, pursuit of power, frenzied activities and busyness, or neurotic acquisition of money to enhance poor self-esteem. Some people might engage in over-indulging their children for their own selfish reasons rather than working to teach them valuable lessons through application of reasonable, fair consequences. When people lose their God-focus, they lose their way.

Throughout the Bible, nation-states and cities have lost their way. The Israelites wandered in the desert for forty years. They lost their sense of direction—physically and spiritually. The Roman Empire took its eyes off its original mission. It lost its previous focus and fell. America has, from time to time, shifted its focus from the mission of her Founders. Our great country now stands at the crossroads of its future. Critical decisions defining America will be made during the next half-decade.

God is omnipresent—meaning He is present everywhere. He is revealed in all of creation. However, it is important to remember that God's creation is not God. His creation is a revelation of Himself—evidence of His awesome greatness. He also revealed

Himself in the Bible. However, His complete and full revelation of Himself is in Jesus Christ. His Spirit does live and move in this world. His Spirit resides inside Christians. Often we might think of God as being up in the sky somewhere and separated from us. However, He dwells through the Holy Spirit inside us. He is an ever-present God—a God of relationship—not a distant God.

When I first noticed the order of the requirements for healing the land, I questioned whether seeking God's presence should have come before the requirement to pray. Then I realized that we seek God's presence through prayer. Although God is omnipresent and we sense Him in many places, it's impossible to connect to Him in relationship except through prayer—a conscious dialogue with our Savior. When we initiate conversation with Him, we are seeking His face. Thus 2 Chronicles 7:14 is stated in exactly the right order—the logical order for the right relationship with God.

In the middle of the night, a member of the opposition sought counsel from Jesus. Nicodemus, a member of the Pharisees, risking intense danger by that meeting, told Jesus that he recognized that He was of God. Jesus replied that no human can see the kingdom of God unless he is spiritually reborn. In other words, a person must refocus from self-centeredness to God-centeredness, humble oneself to God in obedience, and thus experience real personal transformation in order to see the presence of God; i.e., the kingdom of God. (John 3:1-8)

Finding and Experiencing God

Some circumstances in which we can seek and thereby find God are discussed below. Although not exhaustive, these categories represent many situations in which we experience God.

With other believers. Jesus taught that if more than one believer is gathered in His name, He is there with them (Matthew 18:20). He makes a point to be present in a group of Christians. Thus when believers are gathered in worship, we know the presence of God exists. In seeking His presence, it is advisable to worship with others. In so doing, God's presence is magnified.

Through music. Beautiful music touches the soul. Music has a way of bringing forth intense emotions. Poignant contact with God can be made as the Holy Sprit moves in you through hearing harmonious

41

sounds. Certain tonal and rhythmic combinations produce peace. Others induce excitement. Still others produce reverence. Whatever the result, music was created by God to give us a glimpse of eternity.

People who play an instrument tell me that when they are engrossed in their music, they lose touch with their surroundings. It's as if they are suspended in time. I firmly believe that God has created us with the ability to move beyond the three dimensions of the visible world to actually reach out and touch Him in so many ways.

Elaborate music has adorned church and temple life throughout history. The great composers of historical significance wrote their music for divine use, in most cases. An elaborate chorus and orchestra gave impressive performances in the reign of King David. The Hebrews used string, wind, and percussion instruments. Music was a great part of their worship experience. The Ark of the Covenant housed the stone tablets on which were written the Ten Commandments of God to Moses. When King David brought it into Jerusalem, the Ark of the Covenant was transported with great pomp and circumstance—with the accompaniment of "the cornet, and with trumpets, and with cymbals, and making a noise with psalteries and harps." (1 Chronicles 15:28) The cornet was a ram's horn and a psaltery was a lyre. The other instruments in that verse are recognized by the same names today as they were in the time of King David.

The type of music now used in churches reflects cultural experience. Probably the greatest controversy in modern times comes from the Protestant church "music wars." As churches attempt to produce music indigenous to the contemporary culture, some of the laity disagree over what should be "church music." However, instruments used have varied over time. Because each individual has unique taste, today there are multiple choices for worship music. Much of what the laity likes reflects past experience and personal predisposition. Some people consider certain types of music more reverent than others. But from the scriptures, much of the Hebrew music was loud and not very melodious. Thus, obviously one can worship God even with loud clanging, banging, and reverberating cymbals. (Psalm 150:5)

When afflicted by illnesses or enduring physical challenges. My cousin, Gloria Byrd McDonald, has had several illnesses. Each time, the situation seemed almost hopeless. When she was a child, she had a severe case of polio that rendered her a quadriplegic. She eventually regained use of her arms but then had no use of her legs. After intense treatments, she finally strengthened her legs and learned to walk again. She and I have often discussed the long struggle involved in her recovery. As an elementary school child, she didn't fully understand the impact of the illness and remained optimistic—always believing the use of her limbs would return. In her child-mind, all her limbs were *supposed* to work.

However, she tells me that her parents' Godly faith is the key to her recuperation. Her mother was dedicated to her care while her dad worked long days at the shipyards during World War II. Living in California at the time of her polio, her mother, who is my aunt, Ellna Pitts Byrd, tried a risky, controversial new treatment. After having hot packs applied over her body every hour, twelve hours per day, for nine months, plus being involved in therapy directed and managed by her mother, Gloria eventually learned to walk.

Gasoline was being rationed then, in 1943, making transportation difficult. The California health department supplied a three-burner hot plate, number-three wash tub, and a ringer that had to be cranked by hand for squeezing the boiling water from strips of wool blankets used for the treatment packs. Aunt Ellna boiled water for hot packs all day every day—seven days a week—until her hands blistered. She never gave up believing that Gloria could walk. Even now, at age ninety-three, Aunt Ellna still recalls the hardships, fears, challenges, and the constant presence of Almighty God.

In midlife, Gloria decided to change careers. She went back to college and received her degree in nursing. Just a couple of years after becoming an RN, she was stricken with potentially permanent blindness. Medical professionals gave her a one-in-10,000 chance of regaining her sight. After many visits to various ophthalmologists, one pioneer tried an experiment that was successful in halting the progressive sight loss. She was then able to continue her nursing career and served in management positions until retirement. Today, even after experiencing the eye challenges, she maintains her hobby of painting, for which she has won many awards during the last twenty years. She even designed a line of wearable art and art watches which were marketed and sold worldwide. In my opinion, she is an artist who ranks with top-level professionals in her field.

But that's not all. Gloria, three years ago, began having rapid heart palpitations. Upon investigating the cause, she found that she was in imminent danger of suffering a fatal heart attack. Because she had heeded the warning signals, her cardiovascular surgeon was able to interrupt an impending problem through insertion of stents to increase blood flow to her heart. Again, Gloria, with God's help, overcame a medical obstacle.

Although I wasn't alive when Gloria had polio, I watched her go through her other medical issues as well as several other life challenges. She now battles post-polio syndrome daily but keeps courageously active even in constant muscle pain and physical fatigue, although her tiredness isn't obvious. She maintains a full energetic schedule as a community volunteer and is active in her city's political arena. Gloria is a role model for mental toughness and extraordinary endurance.

During all her many medical episodes, never once did she lose her faith. Instead, her medical hardships strengthened her God-trust. She often tells me how God has blessed her life. She definitely has felt His presence in all her illnesses. Gloria has commented that there was no way she could have come through any of these afflictions without the constant companionship of God. She seeks Him regularly and knows that He is a God of miracles. She is a walking, seeing, living example of His awesome greatness.

In celebrations. Jesus had fun. He attended weddings, dined with friends, and teamed up with associates for lively conversation. Once, at a wedding Jesus attended in Cana with His mother and His disciples, the host ran out of wine. So Jesus converted approximately six twenty-gallon jars of water into a fine quality wine. This miracle certainly impressed the wedding guests. (John 2:1-11)

Some people go into deep interpretation of this passage. They somehow determine that the living water of life can be connected to the blood of sacrifice, symbolized by the wine. Others feel that the passage justifies consuming alcoholic beverages at weddings. Maybe John was trying to convey neither interpretation. Perhaps this is a story about Jesus having fun with his family and friends, helping a party host in the kitchen, or pulling a friend out of an embarrassing situation.

Actually, this was a first miracle that caused Jesus' disciples to trust Him. I'm sure they were totally in awe of Him by that feat. The water-into-wine miracle was a precursor to many miracles that followed. The water-to-wine conversion had a purpose. However, it also illustrates a lighter, festive side of Jesus.

Celebrations invite the presence of God. When Christian friends and family are together in celebration of special occasions, the fullness of God abounds. Humor and laughter are good for the soul. Experts indicate that the immune system is fortified by laughter. Internal jogging is what some psychologists call it. Risks of everything from cancer to the common cold can drop when a person blocks time off for clean, wholesome fun on a regular basis.

The birth of a child is a holy experience. When a father and mother see their newborn for the first time, they are emotionally overcome, in most cases, by the petite miracle of life. To think that God could take microscopic matter and create purposeful wonder is beyond human understanding. Scientists probably already hold the capability of cloning humans from DNA. But they can't clone a soul. The "self," the individual soul-identity of a child, is all her own. No scientific lab can produce that. Only God can. When the helpless infant stares into the eyes of his mother for the first time, Mom realizes that she is gazing into the face of Love. God is present right there in her arms. Jesus loved children and proclaimed that His kingdom belonged to them. (Mark 10:14) When holding an innocent child, you are in essence clutching Jesus. You are celebrating God.

Every wholesome celebration is a declaration of life. The joy of living. The gratefulness for the "up" times. Part of the rhythm of the universe. During celebrations, chemical changes actually take place in your body. You can withstand more pain. Depression and sadness lift. You are diverted from the troubles of life. When the celebration is over, the problems seem lighter.

God wants us to revel in healthy fun. In His parable of the son who had left home, squandered his inheritance, and then returned to ask forgiveness (commonly known as the parable of the prodigal son), Jesus told about the great feast the boy's father threw when his son came home. (Luke 15:22-24) This parable represents the celebration in Heaven when someone has pursued his own self-centered path in life and is transformed by shifting his focus from himself to God, then asking for forgiveness for his very human mistakes. God initiates celebration. He wants us to do the same.

In the stages of grief. Loss breeds grief. Anytime we lose something we are attached to or that we love deeply, grief occurs. It is a natural reaction to life change. Shock, anger, guilt, depression, chaos, peace, renewal—all are feelings and perceptions encountered when experiencing bereavement. We can call on God at any stage, and He will comfort us.

I remember that morning well. Three days after Christmas. One day after my birthday. It was 3:05 A.M. My life changed in an instant. My dad had arisen to go to work the early shift at the U.S. Post Office in our small town. Apparently, there was a blood clot closing off blood flow to his heart. When my mother discovered him, he had sat back down on the side of their bed and couldn't talk. I heard my mother scream for me to call an ambulance. I did. I went into their bedroom and helped her lie him back on the bed. I tried to find a pulse rate, to no avail. It was too late when the emergency unit arrived. My dad was dead. As a family, we had gone from the joyful celebration of Christmas and my birthday to the sudden tragedy of death and loss.

I had plenty of time before the emergency team arrived. We lived in a rural area; and in 1967, it took a half-hour to get medical help. We called the neighbors. They came immediately. My head was spinning in chaotic thoughts. I was scared, confused, and in a near state of panic. The shock of being awakened from deep sleep to the unexpected death of my dad was almost overwhelming. During the wait—which seemed like five hours—I slipped into my bedroom closet, got down on my knees, and humbly asked God to get me through all that was ahead. I immediately felt His presence. It surrounded me like a warm blanket. Panic turned to peace.

The years ahead were tumultuous for Mother and me. Finances were limited. Mother, who had always been a homemaker, secured employment. I worked three small jobs in order to have money to finish college and then complete my graduate degree. We owned a farm. Investors would drive the thirty-two miles from Dallas to give us meager offers for the place. They would try to intimidate us into selling our family farm for a pittance.

Although money was tight, we were determined to keep the farm. We loved the place. My dad had loved the place. He had grown up on the farm adjacent to the one we owned. There was no way we were going to let someone buy that homestead at that time! We secured help to work the crops and bring in the seasonal yields. During those challenges, I remember being so tired that sometimes I would sleep for three or four hours at night on the couch in my clothes without ever going to bed—then get up, shower, put on

46

fresh clothes, and begin again. Study and work. That became my life. Through it all, God never left. He walked beside Mother and me all the way. Sometimes He carried both of us. Sometimes He lifted one of us. But He was there all the time.

On clear nights at the farm, I saw God's handiwork in the beautiful stars of a big Texas sky. In the spring of each year, I could sense evidence of His presence in the fragrant pear blossoms in our orchard. He revealed himself in all of nature on our farm. Most of all, I found God in my friends and family. They were so supportive. I couldn't have gotten through all the feelings that grief brings without lots of help from my Christian friends. They never failed. God came to me through them.

King David felt grief. In Psalm 23, David says: "... though I walk through the valley of the shadow of death, I will fear no evil: for Thou art with me ..." The valley of the shadow of death could be depression, sadness, grief, or danger. Whatever the case, David was assured that God was present to comfort, protect, and restore him.

Not only does the loss of someone we love induce grief, but we also encounter bereavement when we lose a job, disaster strikes, or change destroys our comfort zone. I live in one of the fastest-growing counties in the nation. Farmland is being turned into commercial centers. Thousands of houses occupy once peaceful cotton fields and cattle pastures. My city's pioneering families tell me they grieve when developers modernize their family farm. Of course, their grief is softened by the millions of dollars for which they sold the land! But none the less, grief occurs. We grieve for our soldiers killed in war. The whole nation grieved after 9/11. There was sadness for the losses in New York City, Washington, D.C, and for the victims of the plane crash in Pennsylvania. There was also a sense of loss for our open society. Not for many years will Americans feel the safety in public places that we experienced before 9/11. In our anger, depression, fear, and sorrow, God meets us at our point of need. All we must do is ask Him—we must seek His face.

Christians Transport God

As Christians, we carry the face of God with us wherever we go. It is sometimes a daunting realization that we transport the Spirit of

God to various places. It's important to take God into the public arena. You transport Him to work, into the political spectrum if you are involved in local, state, national, or even international politics, to civic organizations, and to club meetings. Wherever you go, you take God with you. Often, you will be the only way the presence of God chooses to enter a place. Christians have an awesome responsibility.

When someone dies, it is important to take God's Spirit to the family. When someone is ill, it is comforting to take God's Spirit to visit her. Sometimes, when someone has cried out to God for help, you might be the answer to that prayer. God may assign you to that person. When your heart breaks for someone in pain—and the sympathy overwhelms you—God is allowing you to feel that person's pain just as He feels it. Don't try to quash your feelings because pain is uncomfortable. Don't deny or avoid it. Confront the reason you feel as you do. Helping the person in pain is likely your assignment.

When you are in intimate, constant communication with God, you will soon recognize His voice. He speaks plainly to those who listen. You will discern a pattern. Sometimes He will prompt you to drive hundreds of miles to a funeral when you are only an acquaintance of that person's family. On another occasion, God may assign you to travel a great distance to attend the high school graduation ceremony for a friend's child. Doing these things makes no logical sense in a busy schedule, but God has other plans for you.

Even when your assignment does seem out-of-the-box or off-the-wall, it is important to pursue it anyway. God's ways aren't human ways. He may be sending you to encourage someone. You may not even be aware that the person needs encouraging. He may urge you to make a phone call to a friend or acquaintance. That call might be just what the other person needs at that time. God knew that individual needed an emotional lift. You didn't. But God chose you to do the job.

When you feel that inner tugging (the Holy Spirit) urging you to do something, do it. Trust your God-instincts. Your presence, your conversation, the knowledge and sensitivity you convey—any of these things may work to heal a person that you had no idea needed help. God uses you to accomplish His purposes.

CHAPTER 5
Focus on Godly Obedience

*You will never feel fully
validated until you find God's
specific purpose for your life.*

The fourth and last of God's requirements for healing our land is stated rather straightforwardly in 2 Chronicles 7:14. The King James version of the Bible declares: "turn from your wicked ways." Other translations use the word "evil" before the word "ways." With this very direct use of language, I get the idea that God is not pleased with human behavior in a term referred to throughout the Bible as "sin." He considers it evil and declares that we must change our focus from sin to salvation in order to save our land. Remember, too, that this message is to God's people—to Christians. We are asked to conduct a self-inventory and take positive action to work with the Holy Spirit in removing sin from our lives. Taking positive action means recognizing our wrongdoing, admitting it to ourselves and God, asking God for forgiveness, and making every effort, with help from the Holy Spirit, to quit the wrongdoing.

Even in today's culture the use of the word "sin" is considered a harsh accusation. I realized that phenomenon several years ago and took a fresh look at the sin that occurs in every human life. No one escapes a deviation from righteousness. No one this side of Jesus

Christ, the only sinless person who ever lived. It is interesting to create conversation on this subject among colleagues. There are varying perspectives. But all come back to the idea that humans do sin.

God created humanity with free will. Thus we have the freedom to sin. Of course, the question usually arises concerning reasons why God allowed sin into the world—even if He did provide freedom of choice. The only reason I can determine is that God wants us to come into His presence, to love Him, because we *wish*—not because we are coerced. He wants us to freely choose obedience to His ways in life. When people are acting positively from free choice, their motives are pure. The results are true. God requires authenticity and truth because He is all truth. He is authentic.

Exploring Sin

In both the Old and New Testaments, sin is considered to be negative, evil behavior. Sin is not just outward violation but is also a state of the heart. In the Bible, the heart is used often to describe the combination of human intent and passion. It is the center of our being. Thus, if you think about sinning, then you have sinned. For example, in Matthew 5:27-28, Jesus says that one of the Ten Commandments demands that God's people avoid adultery. Jesus further stated that if we even visualize involvement in an adulterous situation, we have in turn committed adultery.

Yet Jesus absorbed the sins of all people—past, present, and future—on the cross of Calvary. Because of that act, God offers salvation to all who believe in Jesus Christ, make Him the Leader of their Life, and submit in obedience to His mandates. Jesus' commands for a kingdom-on-earth life with Him are to love God with all our hearts, minds, and souls—and to love other people equal to ourselves. At first sight, that seems simple, but those two statements involve more than just emotional love. Emulating one-way unconditional love, *agape*, God's love (which is supernatural), requires full submission to God and letting go of all self-centered thoughts and behaviors. Doing that is very difficult and can only be accomplished with the help of the Holy Spirit. We cannot accomplish supernatural love by ourselves.

Our sins, or wrongdoings, are covered by God's grace (God's unmerited gift of forgiveness to Christians) if we are sincere followers

50

of Jesus Christ. That doesn't mean that we become Christians with the intent of continuing our wrongdoings and avoiding the commandments of Jesus. It means that we have the will, desire, and intent to follow Him and His ways. Some people view grace as a credit card from God for unlimited intentional wrongdoing. They believe that they can purposefully and repeatedly commit the same sin with no plan of giving up the wrong thought or behavior, and God's grace will keep on covering it. A sincere Christian does the exact opposite. Once she knows God's requirements, she does her best to obey them out of love and gratitude. She endeavors to grow and mature spiritually. As you will read in a later chapter, true faith initiates definite actions. If one defines her own rules, she becomes her own god. It is questionable whether this person ever really intended to make Jesus Christ Leader of her life. There is a great difference between making an emotional response to Christ and making a commitment to Him that is personally transforming.

Yes, we'll slip up from time to time. No person is perfect. God is concerned with our intent. He wants us to *try* to obey. To do so, we must keep on growing spiritually. The objective is to model after the character of Jesus Christ. Many people claim to be believers in Christ but make up their own rules of behavior in violation of the model cast by Jesus Christ. True Christianity requires definite focus on spiritual growth in trying to become more like Jesus. There is a definite difference in recognizing intellectually the historical Jesus and submitting your life unconditionally to Jesus. The Bible states that the latter is required. (Luke 9:23-26)

Sin hurts others, and it hurts us. It causes a "spiritual disconnect." When we are spiritually disconnected, it is impossible to feel the presence of God. When we deviate from the path proclaimed by Jesus Christ, God seems distant. In other words, the Bible tells us that we cannot see the kingdom of God if our view is blocked by sin. Relationships are destroyed, lives are lost, tragic accidents happen, wars are fought—often as a result of human sin.

Soul In Need

I can grasp the idea of sin much better when I view it as an acrostic, S-I-N. That, in my mind, stands for Soul In Need. The real cause of our sin occurs when we try to solve our problems in a self-centered way as opposed to God's way. Each person is born by design with three holes in his soul. I have been using the concept of "holes in the soul" for several years. I also read recently in *The Complete Life Encyclopedia* by Frank Minirth, M.D., Paul Meier, M.D., and Stephen Arterburn, M. Ed. (Nashville, Tennessee: Thomas Nelson Publishers, 1995) that Dr. Meier also talks about holes in the soul. Use of these terms by both of us is purely coincidental and bears different definitions in the context of our individual research.

Most of our motives for doing anything in life result from trying to fill these three holes. It is in trying to pursue a self-centered path to filling those holes that causes one to sin. The three holes are a result of three human needs: the need for safety, the need for community, and the need for validity. God has solutions for all three of these needs. However, humans usually try to find their own ways of fulfilling these wants before turning to God for the answers. Many people never turn to the one true God for solutions. Instead, they choose either to pursue false gods and/or intentionally inflict evil. And we know from Biblical scripture that evil is real and does indeed exist.

The need for safety. In college classes on the psychology of human motivation, students learn that there is a hierarchy of needs. Abraham Maslow was a famous psychologist who designed this model. Many other experts have since built on his work. Maslow indicated that the first need of every human is for physical and psychological safety. If we don't feel safe, we can't move away from that feeling of insecurity.

Juan and Roberto were traveling on Interstate Highway 20 a few miles west of Midland, Texas. It was a blustery May afternoon. Having just negotiated the deal of a lifetime for their building company, of which each was a 50 percent owner, they were in an ecstatic mood. They calculated that they would make millions of dollars in profits over the next three years. As they were in animated conversation excitedly discussing various subcontractors who could contribute expertise to this major project, Roberto noticed an ominous cloud approaching from the southwest. Suspecting hard rain and high winds, he started looking for a place to find shelter. It was about 5:00 P.M., so Juan and Roberto decided to take the next exit and grab a bite to eat at All You Can Eat Home Cooking.

As they stepped outside their truck, the air seemed warm to the point of being sticky. The humidity was obviously high on this 97 degree West Texas day. Discounting the buildup of dark clouds in the southwest, the two men entered the crowded restaurant. Apparently the place was popular. The food was good; the price was right. As Juan and Roberto surveyed the restaurant crowd before being seated, they noticed that everyone was busily involved in their own intimate conversations—seemingly unaware of the other people around them. The acoustics weren't the best, so the combination of all voices blended into a dull roar.

The waitress soon seated the two fellows, handed them a thick menu listing everything from chicken fried steak to grilled salmon along with pictures of scrumptious desserts obviously loaded with calories. Juan and Roberto's conversation turned to the various items on the menu—discussing what was good and what they might bypass. Juan had eaten at this place several times before and could identify the winners and losers on the menu. Roberto had never been there. The gentlemen decided on the large chicken fried steak, iced tea, and a slice of coconut pie topped with one-inch meringue for each of them. They then nodded to the waitress that they were ready to order their meal.

Before the waitress could approach their table, there was a loud roar coming from the southwest. Looking out the window, Juan and Roberto noticed that the sky was colored in shades ranging from dark green to black. Suddenly, hail hit. It hammered the rooftop for ten minutes, then stopped abruptly. The winds ceased. The calm before the storm. Then came a sound as if a train were speeding directly into the restaurant. The roar was deafening. A Texas tornado! People dove under tables. The roof caved in. Power poles fell into the restaurant. Debris flew everywhere. Fear gripped Juan and Roberto as they waited under the table for the tornado to pass.

Within a few minutes, all was quiet. Hard rain had begun to fall. The place was soaked. Electric wires were lying all around the premises. Frightening! When the guys decided that the tornado was definitely over, they crawled through the piles of roof shingles, insulation, and shattered glass while carefully avoiding the electric lines, to the outside street where they could get a good look back on the restaurant to survey the damage.

When they scrambled to their feet and looked toward the eating establishment they had just exited, they could hear faint cries for help. "Someone, anybody, help me! I can't move my legs," cried a voice from the debris. They could hear the screams of babies under the rubble. Crowds had begun to gather, and the fire department had arrived. Juan and Roberto ran over to the fire chief and asked how they could help in pulling people from the devastation.

The late afternoon wore on. The sun came out to signify hope as it always does after a Texas tornado. The skies turned pure blue as if nothing had happened just an hour before. Dusk fell. Then darkness. Not all the people had been accounted for. Juan and Roberto worked feverishly with the volunteers throughout the night until noon the next day. All the people in the restaurant were finally found. Two dead. Eleven wounded. Everyone else was all right. Shaken. Shocked. But all right.

Exhausted, Juan and Roberto went to find the truck they had driven to the restaurant nineteen hours before. It was not on the parking lot. The violent, swirling winds must have moved it to another place. But where?

This story illustrates how rapidly humans can change from higher-level wants and needs to seeking basic safety. Just minutes before the tornado, Juan and Roberto were excitedly discussing a multi-million dollar company project. In a matter of seconds, their ecstasy changed to horror. They were no longer concerned about money. Their full attention was focused on survival. Maslow's theory argues that we can be at the top of the hierarchy in the stage of self-fulfillment at one moment and then fall to the bottom rung of safety needs in an instant. Juan and Roberto demonstrated this phenomenon. Safety needs are basic.

Psychological safety needs are also basic. People want to feel safe. If one feels that her parents are too busy for her, she begins to develop psychological insecurities. When one spouse abuses the other, the abused partner feels unsafe. In cases of divorce, many children report feelings of insecurity. There may be fear that the divorce is their fault. Children may be afraid that the other parent will abandon them and render them homeless. People fear running out of money in old age. Some individuals fear being alone. Others vie for the top position in a corporation to assure maximum power because they fear facing life without strong stamina. Psychological insecurities abound.

While trying to save ourselves in situations where physical safety is in danger, we often cry out to God for protection. As we are waiting for the threat to pass, we do all we can to assist ourselves and pray to God to perform a miracle and/or give us wisdom to know how to extricate ourselves from the danger. On a national level, prayer sessions are often held for seeking God's guidance and wisdom—and protection. It is important to have strong military might, law enforcement, and intelligence capabilities for a nation's safety. However, these systems, sophisticated as they might be, are human-driven and by definition of being "human" are subject to errors. Sometimes these errors can be fatal. Dependence on these systems alone without consideration of God's contribution is insufficient.

God is still in the design details and is also in the conditions under which these means are applied. Sometimes, a law enforcement officer stops an individual for speeding. That person turns out to be a wanted terrorist. Weather conditions can cause some of the best defensive designs to fail. These seemingly coincidental events may actually be orchestrated by God. He is our nation's ultimate Protector. He can shield our country from harm or lift His protection. In 2 Chronicles 7:14, the scripture indicates that God's actions directly relate to the prayers and obedience of His people.

In cases where psychological safety is threatened, we often try to handle the situations without God's help. We may turn to the quest for power, greed for money, performance for attention, anorexia, bulimia, alcohol abuse, pornography, adultery, or over-dependency on other people—to name a few self-directed (and misdirected) attempts at solutions. We replace God-answers with our own answers. When we seek our own self-directed path to psychological safety without involving God, we usually commit sin as a result of our soul's need.

The need for community. God created humans with a relational goal in mind. Christians believe that God is a Holy Trinity. He is one in three—Father (God the Creator and Master Intelligence), Son (Jesus), and Holy Spirit (God's spirit). Humanity is designed to relate to God and to one another. God's commandments and those of Jesus are prescribed to maximize relationships with the Holy Trinity and to one another. Flawlessly obeying Jesus' commands would result in perfect peace and harmony. However, humans aren't capable of perfection on this earth. There will never be complete accord and unanimity in this life.

55

Nevertheless, all humans have the need to belong to a group at some level. They want *to love* and *to be loved*. Belonging to a community promotes the feeling of security and safety people so desperately need. Community needs, however, establish belongingness. That is a higher-level need than safety. It is less basic. Until safety needs are met, people do not pursue community needs. When people feel disconnected, there is lack of intimacy. When that emotional closeness is lacking, people are driven to fulfill the need.

Halene is thirty-five years of age. She feels empty. And she hasn't a clue why she feels that way. She can be in a large crowd and still feel lonely. She has been in and out of serious relationships with men, but none of them seem to work out. She would really like to find a husband, get married, and have a family. But life doesn't seem to be pointing in that direction for her right now. Halene cannot understand why she develops such close relationships with people only to have them backfire in her face most of the time.

Born to two struggling college students in their early twenties, Halene experienced the workaholism of both parents from the beginning of her life. Her parents both studied hard and pursued graduate work. Her dad then went to medical school and acquired his M.D. After that achievement, he was in tremendous debt. He left for work early and returned home late every day while building his medical practice. Halene's mother was a rising business executive who found her work both challenging and fulfilling. Her parents felt that Halene had the best care possible from the live-in nanny they hired to attend to her every need.

As a youngster, Halene could never quite understand why her nanny accompanied her to most school activities and held most of the conferences with her teachers. Yes, Halene's parents attended her recitals, soccer games, and school-sponsored activities when possible. But it wasn't possible very often. Her nanny conducted most of the child-rearing practices. At approximately age eight, Halene began to question her importance to her parents. After all, they rarely gave her their time. They must not care for her very much, she reasoned. She yearned to have her mother home when she returned from school each day. She begged her dad to coach her soccer team. To no avail. They reasoned with her that she had more than most children. They loved her and gave her everything she wanted, they told her repeatedly. Still, Halene felt empty and abandoned. She loved her nanny but longed for intimacy with her parents.

Halene often visited the home of her friend, Holly, whose house was modest and much smaller than that of Halene and her family. Holly's mom drove a car that was six years old, and her dad commuted to work in an older four-wheel-drive vehicle. Because of family financial limitations, Holly couldn't be in all the extracurricular activities in which Halene was involved. The elaborate vacations that were common to Halene's family eluded Holly's folks. Yet, when Halene entered Holly's home, she felt surrounded by emotional warmth. She felt wrapped in coziness. The house always smelled of something freshly baked—or maybe just coffee brewing. Holly's two brothers were usually in the backyard with friends playing on the swings or in the fort their dad had built for them. Halene loved to visit Holly. She felt so welcome. She came alive with Holly's family. Quickly, Halene recognized that money didn't buy connectedness; and wonderful careers couldn't substitute for family life.

Halene became too attached to Holly's family. She wanted to be with them all the time. She became jealous when Holly invited other friends to visit. Halene wanted the love and intimacy that being Holly's friend offered. When she found out that Holly had several good friends, Halene distanced herself from Holly. She wanted to be Holly's only friend. After all, she would do anything for Holly. Halene was offended that Holly didn't seem to reciprocate those feelings to the same degree.

When Halene reached her teen years, she quickly became sexually active. She had learned in Sunday school at an early age that sex outside marriage was wrong. But, when she was engaged in that activity, she felt so needed and wanted. In fact, she always seemed to choose young men with some unresolved problems so that she could feel strong by continually helping them with their life challenges. Their weakness made her feel strong. It seemed, however, that just as the relationship grew extremely close, the boy would leave. Most of her boyfriends told her that she demanded too much—that she was a clinging vine who smothered them.

The clinging became controlling. Finally, Halene found it hard to establish relationships with anyone. She tried too hard and demanded too much. Friends grew tired of the hard work and stress of being Halene's friend. Thus, at age thirty-five, Halene is very lonely and still unmarried. She has no close friends.

What happened to Halene? Where did she go wrong? Halene obviously has a great need for community, intimacy and connectedness. In their own way, her parents loved her, but they were extremely self-centered and loved their work more for the personal rewards it provided. They demonstrated that. Halene figured it out at an early age and began to desperately search for someone to fill the loneliness that she felt deep inside her soul. Instead of seeking God, holding conversations with Him, admitting her weakness and seeking His strength, she made other people her gods and expected them to provide her with help they weren't capable of giving her. She also tried to overpower people with control and pushiness. She enjoyed other people's weaknesses because those types made her feel strong. She lived in self-denial and self-deception. She tried to satisfy her needs in a self-centered way.

Anytime we miss God's way, we become self-centered, and sin results. When we seek to obey God and solve our problems by consulting Him, we can become a part of His community of believers. We can participate in a local church. That institution is divinely designed to offer a loving community. If yours doesn't, find one that does. In that community, you can find the help you need by consulting a pastor or professional Christian counselor, belonging to a small group, or working with a caring mentor among the laity. People in the church will help hold you accountable for your healing process. God, through relationships with Christians who care for you, will relieve the longing to rid yourself of that lonely hollow feeling which results from your unfulfilled need for community.

Halene is just one example of a person's attempt to fill her connection needs by doing it her way. People may suffer from guilt—and cover the guilt with drugs. Other individuals may be depressed and unhappy and attempt to solve their problems with engagement in sexual misconduct or over-indulgence in alcohol. Perfectionism is a miserable problem suffered by thousands of people, some of whom may try to resolve that plight through eating disorders. In some instances, young people try to find connectedness by joining a youth gang. In more extreme cases, people might join terrorism cells in search for belongingness, a sense of personal importance, and passion for a cause. Anytime we self-direct a remedy for a Soul

In Need (SIN) problem and eliminate God's prescription, we will take a wrong, painful, harmful path. When we harm ourselves, we in turn harm others who love us. People might even harm strangers if they drive drunk and are involved in an accident, join gangs, or participate in terror groups, for example. When sin affects one person, it likely forces collateral damage on others.

The need for validity. People want to feel important. They wish to be considered valuable. Many individuals today are searching for purpose, yet so many are wandering generalities. They have no clue about their life-mission. In seeking to validate themselves, folks often try to become important in the eyes of others. When self-importance is the motive, humans enter a never-ending cycle. Validity addictions often happen to people when they continually try to maintain their public stature. The more important they perceive themselves to be, the more important they try to become. The power they feel from their prominence causes them to desire it even more. So they enter a vicious cycle.

They then become so self-absorbed (in extreme cases) that they alienate friends and family. This intensive need-satisfaction cycle started with the quest for validity due to poor self-esteem. Humans who become involved in this never-ending pursuit eventually discover the futility of seeking importance outside God's validation process.

God has already validated His people. In Psalm 139:13-14, David states that God respectfully and wonderfully made him. Similarly, God has a purpose for each of His people. God told the prophet Jeremiah that He had plans for his success. (Jeremiah 29:11) The scripture further depicted that God provided His people with hope and protection from harm. Those promises made in ancient times to Jeremiah carry forward to all Christians today. God's guarantee never changes. He is the same today as He was in the beginning. God's character never alters its course. (Malachi 3:6)

You will never feel fully validated until you find God's specific purpose for your life. Strangely, when you discover your life-purpose, all three holes in your soul will be filled. You will feel safe, connected, and validated. The macro-purpose for every Christian is to emulate the character of Jesus Christ. However, the micro-purpose for every Christian is to pursue individual God-assignments. Through prayer and meditation, reading the scriptures, listening for God's instructions, seeking wise counsel, monitoring the circumstances in which you find yourself, talking with other Christians, and auditing your natural talents and spiritual gifts, you will eventually discover why you are here. Then God may direct you into special preparation for your life-work. You may be asked to gain particular experience or pursue additional education. Most of the time, God doesn't have just one magnificent purpose in mind for our lives. He uses the humbly committed Christian in various assignments throughout the individual's time on earth.

However, God usually builds on skills you already possess and on the experiences you have already had. He doesn't waste time or effort. He has been grooming you all along for your particular assignment. That assignment will then prepare you for your next point of service. If you continue to listen to His voice, you will be drawn from place to place, person to person, and task to task in God's plan. When you are on God's path, you will never feel empty, unimportant, detached, or lonely. Your soul will be in a state of pure joy and purpose—even when problems arise and hardships occur. Walking through life focused on God's way provides supernatural strength and power to overcome any obstacle. That's part of God's guarantee.

Section 3

God's Promises to the
United States of America

CHAPTER 6

God Hears Our Prayers from Heaven

In His way and in His perfect time,
God answers all prayers sincerely
and humbly requested of Him.

Today, as I write this chapter, there is great celebration in Salt Lake City, Utah. Teenager Elizabeth Smart, who was kidnapped nine months ago in the middle of the night at knifepoint from her bedroom, has been found and returned home safely. The homecoming was broadcast nationwide by a wide variety of media. When Elizabeth's father, Ed Smart, held a news conference, he emphasized that many people had been praying for his daughter's safe return, and that those prayers had been answered.

God promises to hear our prayers—all prayers. But He sets certain conditions on our prayers. They must be humble, persistent, and according to God's will, not selfish requests for accomplishing our own goals and ambitions prayed with arrogance and timetables set for God. Under God's prescribed conditions, He answers our prayers in His own way and in His own perfect time with the result that is best in the long term for His kingdom. Jesus' brother, James, wrote in his letter to Jewish Christians scattered throughout the Mediterranean area (James 4:3) that prayers are not answered when people ask with the wrong motives.

No doubt all of us have experienced answers to prayers. However, some people see no need to pray. They feel that if God is all-powerful and all-knowing, He has everything figured out for their lives already, and prayer won't change anything. If He has a purpose for us, they reason, then we are completely guided by Him. They question: Why should we intervene?

The answer to the above question is complicated. Yes, God does have a plan for everyone—a purpose for each person. However, we must stay in constant conversation with Him to stay "on purpose." It is true that God is all-knowing. And yes, He knows what we are going to ask before we ask. He knows our needs before we discover and express them. He knows how our lives are going to turn out and the very day on which we will die. But our prayers still count. Because we are free-willed, we have the power to change things provided that our requests are within God's will for the long-term good of His kingdom. On most occasions, God depends on our initiative to affect events. He knows what we are going to do. Prayer works for clarity in our own minds as well as for conversation with God. God is daily as well as long-term. His ways are not our ways, and we will never be able to explain His ways as long as we dwell on this earth. He asks us to accept His character on faith. And our success in life is dependent on our degree of faith. (Matthew 9:29)

God's promise to answer prayer is found in Jeremiah 33:3. If His people call on Him, He promises to answer. Again, Matthew expresses the power of prayer, persistence, and action in the will of God. (Matthew 7:7-12) However, answers will come in His way and in His time. He can see the future and what's best for us long-term; we cannot. The wisdom expressed in Isaiah 40:31 promises energy and renewed strength to those who patiently wait upon the Lord's timing.

Answered Prayers

I have three, perhaps four, cousins who contracted polio in 1943 and 1944. I was not yet born but began hearing their story at a very early age from various family members. Because I was a small child in the early 1950s, when people were terrified of the paralysis and death inflicted by polio, I was always poignantly affected every time someone would tell me about the time my three cousins faced that killer disease.

On a hot summer afternoon in 1943 at our grandfather's farm, some of my cousins were playing near the tank in the field behind the big farm house. Several of my aunts, uncles, and their families along with my parents and grandparents had gathered for a reunion. The adults were visiting inside the house while the children explored the farm. Without the knowledge of their parents, the children decided to go wading in the farm's shallow stock tank. After their explorations and play time, they returned to the house and all seemed well. Several days later, after proceeding to their respective homes, two of the children began to have headaches and high fever.

One cousin survived without any lasting harmful effects. Because he had such a light case, there is only suspicion that he had contracted the disease. The other cousin, Gloria, about whom you read in an earlier chapter, had a severe case of polio. The source of the disease was not identified as the farm stock tank because the parents never knew until much later that the children went wading in it.

Early the next summer, in 1944, some of my cousins were again visiting my grandfather's farm. While they were there, a letter arrived from my Aunt Ellna in California stating that Gloria had defied all the odds and was walking. The family was very excited by the wonderful news—especially my cousin, Frances Haydon (later Frances Haydon Parnell). She ran to my mom and dad's house about an eighth of a mile down the road to announce to my parents the great news about Gloria. The entire family celebrated all weekend. Polio was such a debilitating disease that walking after being a quadriplegic was a real miracle.

Two sisters contract polio. Not knowing that the farm's stock tank was probably the source of the polio virus, Frances and her sister, Charlotte Haydon (now Charlotte Haydon Smith), waded in the water as all my young cousins did when they visited the farm. After later returning home to El Paso, they had both contracted the dreadful disease by late July. I can only imagine the intensity under which my aunt, Nell Pitts Haydon, mother of Charlotte and Frances, operated through that critical time. She hired a babysitter and cook to care for Charlotte during the day while she stayed with Frances in the hospital. Other extended family members helped with Frances at night. To compound her situation, Aunt Nell was pregnant with her third child during the polio episode. Frances had a very severe case of polio and was a paraplegic for the remainder of her life. She died several years ago from complications of diabetes and heart disease—probably resulting, in some measure, from being wheelchair-bound for most of five decades.

Charlotte was four years of age when she was stricken with polio. She recovered, but her back began to curve at age sixteen due to the residual effects of the disease. She had surgery to correct the spinal curve and was in a full body cast for a period of time. Charlotte remembers her mother's courage during these very trying times. She said: "Mother was a total optimist who always made each of us feel that we could accomplish anything. Several times, well-meaning but uninformed people would say hurtful things by suggesting that Frances and I were ill because of our parents' sins. Mother would just smile and explain to us that such was not the case. She always emphasized to us that God was good and that our polio was an obstacle that would make us grow stronger spiritually and closer to Him as a result. I never felt that I was handicapped or different. Mother always motivated me to feel that I could do anything."

Because Charlotte was small in stature, most colleges rejected her applications to their nursing schools stating that she was too petite to carry out rigorous nursing duties. With dogged determination, she persisted. Finally, a Catholic school in Waco, Texas, accepted her. While attending that institution, she studied pediatrics and psychiatry at an affiliated college in New Orleans, Louisiana. She graduated with honors and worked as an RN for thirty-four years before retiring from the profession a few years ago. During her career in nursing, she received many honors. Charlotte authored several articles, which were published in professional journals and won various national awards, as well as training films and patient education materials. Still somewhat involved in her career, she is now a part-time clinical instructor for surgical technology students at a local community college. During her dedicated search for a college to attend, she remembered her mother's teachings about being able to do anything she wished with God's help. During her career as a nurse, she would often pray with patients while holding their hands prior to surgery.

Periodically, Charlotte has continued to have back and neck trouble. In September 2001 she had neck surgery and was doing well. About 4:00 A.M. the following morning, she quit breathing. Eventually, because of complications when trying to revive her, she was placed on a ventilator in ICU. The prognosis was very guarded. If she lived, the doctors told her family she could be brain dead, be forced to remain on the ventilator, or be comatose for the remainder of her life. She could even have a stroke. The situation looked grim.

Prayer chains were formed through the area churches and in the churches of immediate and extended family members. Family and friends prayed. Pastors of area churches came to the hospital and spent time with the family. Chaplains stopped by and prayed. The anesthesiologist who was with Charlotte in surgery also prayed with the family prior to surgery and continually prayed for Charlotte after her situation became critical.

Then the medical staff began to decrease the sedation to see if Charlotte could regain consciousness and to check for residual damage. She opened her eyes and saw her family. She smiled but was too weak to even raise her hand to all the people who were standing at her bedside. No brain damage. No stroke. No permanent damage of any kind. God had produced a miracle. Hundreds of prayers had been answered.

Mac's five-year challenge. Charlotte emphatically believes that prayer changes things. Her husband, Mac Smith, had kidney failure and was in need of a kidney transplant. On dialysis three times per week for five years while waiting on a kidney, he was on church prayer lists throughout Texas. Prayers for him were lifted up regularly by friends, family, and strangers alike. His son was a match for a kidney donation, but Mac refused the kidney, thinking that his son could be genetically predisposed to his problem and might need that kidney himself one day. Being such an unselfish father, Mac risked death rather than endanger his son's future.

While on dialysis, Mac continued to work in the air conditioning and heating business he owned. In the hot summers he would crawl through sweltering attics. On 100 degree days he drove with his truck windows up and without air conditioning. This caused him to perspire more in order to reduce his body fluids. During this five-year period of kidney failure, Mac restricted his liquids because his kidneys were not able to rid his body of fluids, thus causing the potential for congestive heart failure. Mac would work in the mornings and have dialysis for three and one-half hours in the required afternoons. A very strict diet was required. Mac's skin itched constantly due to his high degree of phosphorus accumulation since his failed kidneys weren't able to excrete this important mineral. Yet he worked daily. Mac had a fistula procedure in his arm, which had to be protected. Any nick in the skin over the fistula would cause him to bleed to death. Because of the danger, he always carried a tourniquet with him.

That regular routine continued for five years. It took a lot of faith in God to carry on for those long years without becoming discouraged. Prayers continued. Mac's supporters persisted. Then one day the call came. A cadaver kidney was available. Mac and Charlotte drove the 200 miles to Baylor Hospital in Dallas, Texas, where the transplant took place. After the surgery, recovery was tough. An episode of suspected kidney rejection occurred. But Mac survived. Nine years later, Mac is thriving.

Mac and Charlotte are truly two of my family heroes. They inspire me beyond belief. Their constant, tough-minded faith in God, sense of humor, and high degree of optimism repeatedly have modeled Christian courage to me and other family members. Mac and Charlotte feel that prayer has sustained them through many brutal situations. Charlotte claims that God answers all prayers in His time. As is evident from their example, patience, persistence, and strong faith are essential in living life purposed by God's plan.

When Prayers Seem Unanswered

Most of the cases I've mentioned throughout this book have resulted in successful outcomes. The majority of the prayers were answered in ways that people requested. But what about Charlotte's sister, Frances, who made requests to God and her paralysis continued? What about parents who prayed for the safe return of their kidnapped children to no avail? What about families who prayed for the return of soldiers from war only to receive notice that they had been killed in action? What about times when you have prayed and experienced no apparent results? Did those prayers go unanswered?

We are promised that if we humbly petition for God's will to be done, our prayers will be answered. We then must suppose that when those requests are followed, then God does answer prayers. Remember that we pray for God's will—meaning that He answers His way, not our way. He answers for the long-term good of His kingdom. In Gethsemane, Jesus prayed for God's will; and Jesus died a cruel death on the cross to accomplish God's purpose for His life on earth.

Perhaps a person does not recover from a crippling disease because her role in God's kingdom is to inspire countless numbers of people to be spiritually strong. As they watch her example of Godly courage, they apply it to their own lives. For example, my cousin, Frances, used her paraplegia as a motivator for helping paralyzed people adapt to their life challenges through her appearances in rehabilitation training films she made for Baylor Hospital in Dallas, which were used at Mayo Clinic. In spite of nine major surgeries and spending, collectively, three of the first seven years after the onset of her polio in the hospital, she attended public schools and earned a community college degree when there were no ramps for the disabled. Someone always had to lift her up steps unless she had on leg braces.

On the days when she wore braces, Frances had to climb steps backward. But that didn't deter her. Slowly, she struggled her way to the top. She battled and won at many other things in life just as she conquered climbing the stairs. Frances obtained a driver's license and drove a car, owned her own home, had a full career, got married, and adopted a beautiful baby girl. In spite of all her difficulties and challenges, she lived a fully productive life and inspired many paraplegics to do the same.

Often, too, when children have been kidnapped and not returned alive, the surviving parents turn their grief into positive energy by starting nationwide programs designed to save great numbers of other children. When relatives have been killed by drunk drivers or have died of cancer, family members initiate foundations or campaign for the passage of specific laws to save other lives. God takes tragedy and turns it into triumph through willing participants in His master plan. When we suffer losses or pain of any kind, good results can happen long-term if we are yielded to God's will.

God doesn't promise that we will never suffer loss, that we will never cry barrels of tears, or live throughout life with healthy bodies. He asks us to live for His kingdom. To have great faith. To persist in His promises of comfort and the assurance that He is with us every step of the way. He never asks us to bear more than we can carry with the help He provides. In His way and in His perfect time, God answers all prayers sincerely and humbly requested of Him.

God Hears from Heaven

God guarantees that He will hear from Heaven, His dwelling place. Does that mean that God is "out there" somewhere? That He is distant and separate from us? Some religions believe that God is distant and separate. Christians, however, believe that God's spirit resides within us and that Heaven is near. Heaven, according to Jesus, is a place (John 14:2) and a spiritual residence. It is an eternal kingdom. (2 Peter 1:11) In Heaven, there is no evil; joy abounds; and there is no suffering. But Heaven is not distant. It is something that we can experience, in part, right here on earth. When we become a Christian, our soul is sealed by the Holy Spirit. (Ephesians 1:13-14) We have access to a piece of Heaven within us. In the Lord's Prayer, Jesus suggested that Heaven could come to earth. When Jesus walked the earth, Heaven came down. After He arose, the Holy Spirit was available as a Comforter. Thus Heaven is available to all Christians now. However, only after death will we reside with God and Jesus in that perfect place called Heaven.

Jesus referred to the kingdom of Heaven (or kingdom of God) in his teachings. He said it was not of this world. (John 18:36) Paul recognized that it is spiritual and about right living and joy in the Holy Spirit. (Romans 14:17) To enter, we must have the faith of a little child (Matthew 18:3), claimed Jesus.

Wherever God is (and Jesus is on His right hand), there Heaven is. In this dwelling place close to our hearts, God hears and answers our prayers according to His perfect will.

CHAPTER 7

God Forgives

Forgiveness begins with a decision
to change your way of thinking
about another person or situation.

When God forgives our sins, He also forgets them. It's as if they never happened. Forgiveness, which is the emotional release of wrongdoings with no intent to retaliate, is God's prerogative and an important part of His guarantee. In Psalm 130, the writer is passionately asking God for mercy, knowing that God is the source of all hope and unconditional love. The author cites that no one would be left standing if God kept a record of all sins and never redeemed His people. Tremendous insight.

In 2 Chronicles 7:14, which we have been studying throughout this book, as well as in Luke 17:3-4, forgiveness is based on repentance; i.e., actually feeling sorry in your innermost being for your wrong and turning away from the wrongdoing. In 2 Chronicles 7:14, God promises to forgive their sins after His people repent. In Luke 17:3-4, Jesus tells his disciples to always be willing to forgive people each time they repent of their sins. There is no indication in these two passages that forgiveness happens without the perpetrator's repentance.

The unmerciful servant. In the parable of the unmerciful servant, Jesus told the story of a servant who owed the king a very large sum of money. When the king wanted to collect the debt from the servant, the man had no money for repayment. The king was going to sell the servant and his family along with his possessions in order to raise money to collect the debt. The servant begged the king for mercy. Mercy was granted. The servant left and pursued a peer who owed him a small sum of money. When the debtor begged the servant for mercy, the fellow servant had his peer thrown into prison. When the king heard about the unforgiving servant, he had him hauled into jail until his debt was paid.

The moral to this parable of Jesus in Matthew 18:21-35 is that God forgives us to the degree that we forgive others. Our debts to God are huge because of our daily sins; and He is willing to forgive us if we turn away from our wrongdoings. People's debts to us pale in comparison to what we owe God. Yet some of us are unwilling to forgive even the smallest of sins against us. God notices and will compensate us likewise.

The philosophy of Jesus. Jesus further makes the same point in His Sermon on the Mount (Matthew 5:7) when he states that the merciful are happy because they will obtain mercy. In the Lord's Prayer (Matthew 6:12), Jesus prays to His Father that we will be forgiven by God equal to how we forgive others. Here is an example of the principle of sowing and reaping. If we sow forgiveness, then we will reap forgiveness. If we sow anger, revenge, and bitterness, then we will receive those negative consequences in return.

Alan's plight. Alan was the oldest child in a family of seven children. His mom was a vocational nurse, and his dad labored as a plumber. Each child in the family had a responsibility in the household; and as soon as each person was old enough, he would secure a job to help with the family finances. Alan started mowing lawns in his neighborhood at age ten. Each summer he would secure more lawns to mow until he had a sizable spring and summer income from his enterprise by the time he was sixteen years old. As a teenager, during the school year, he would work afternoons and weekends at Cluck and Chick fast food restaurant.

With all this labor in his life, he had little time to study and minimal time for a social life. Alan, however, was happy to be earning a good income because he could help his family as well as make payments on his new Mustang convertible. Of course, he also had to cover monthly insurance premiums on his car. But he always managed to have enough money in that he was willing to work hard. Because of his success as an entrepreneur, Alan set a goal of going to college and majoring in business administration with the ultimate objective of achieving an MBA and then forming his own company. While mowing lawns, he would daydream about the business he would own some day and the lifestyle he would lead when he became rich and successful.

Then the unthinkable happened. During geometry class, the high school principal knocked on the classroom door and asked to speak to Alan. When Alan met the principal in the hall, he told Alan that his dad had been in an automobile accident and was at the local hospital's emergency room. Alan immediately went to the hospital to be with his dad. The injuries were debilitating. Spinal cord injury. Probably permanent. Alan was devastated. His life changed at that moment. His dad spent many months in rehabilitation and could never return to work as a plumber. The accident was his dad's fault, so there was no way to collect damages. Alan's mother began working fewer hours as a nurse in order to be at home caring for Alan's father.

Life was tough. Alan took an additional job to help even more than before with the family's financial obligations. He sold his beloved Mustang and bought a pre-owned clunker just for minimal transportation needs. He fell behind in school and barely graduated. With such low grades, Alan decided to continue living at home and not attend college. He felt obligated to help his parents make ends meet and aid his brothers and sisters in finishing high school.

Alan's despair. Fast forward two decades. Now Alan is thirty-eight years old. He is bitter. His two marriages have ended in divorce. He is not close to his three children because they feel he is full of rage and is verbally abusive. He has difficulty relating well with his coworkers. Life seems to be going downhill for him. Nothing is working out as he dreamed it would when he was a teenager. He is angry at his brothers and sisters. He is resentful of his dad. Alan believes that he has gotten the worst that life has to offer.

73

Alan has a forgiveness problem. After his dad was involved in the debilitating accident, Alan felt obligated to help the family financially. He gave up his social life, his car, and his future plans. As time marched on, Alan became very angry at the situation. Life had dumped on him, he determined. His family never went to church. Alan wasn't a Christian and had never pondered forgiveness very much. Not being in tune with his emotions, the only outlet he felt was rage. Hurts were expressed as hostility. Frustration was vented as rage. Everything turned to bitterness and anger. Then the depression hit. His anger turned inward, and Alan felt the deep, wrenching pain of despair. *My life is over,* he thought. *Nothing to live for anymore.*

Alan had never determined that he was angry at his family because he felt they took valuable parts of his life from him. Therefore he could never understand that he had to forgive them and move on. Instead, he kept wallowing in his anger and resentment until he ruined every relationship he had. Because he didn't have a relationship with God, Alan didn't seek forgiveness from Him. The thought never occurred to him. He was miserable. Then a coworker recognized his symptoms and invited him to a Bible study group on anger management which was being facilitated by a Christian counselor. Alan was so desperate and depressed that he was ready to do almost anything to get relief. He went to the group meeting.

Alan's discovery. Much to his surprise, the lessons weren't concerned with how to seek revenge. They were on self-examination. The emphasis was on approaching people from the past, living and dead, and discussing the problem with them (if living), reconciling if possible, but in the end forgiving them—all of them. Alan applied the principles. He talked with his siblings and mother. He visited the cemetery and "talked" with his dad. He looked up his former wives and talked with them. His children agreed to meet with him. With the help of his Bible study group, Alan discerned a behavior pattern: Internalized anger. Inability to forgive.

At 2:00 A.M. after a night of tossing and turning, Alan petitioned God for help. Peace came over him. He asked God to change his life. Alan gave his life to God and promised to walk by faith down whatever path God led him. Then Alan went about the hard work of forgiveness. Instead of having a constant pity-party, Alan chose to attend night classes at the local community college. He made great grades. Then he finished his last two years at the university in the city forty miles away. His life straightened out. The anger and bitterness turned to peace. His relationships prospered. He is now married and has a baby. When Alan learned to forgive, and asked God to forgive him, he was healed from a lifetime of hurt.

God forgave us first through Jesus Christ. However, we must access Christ through faith and obedience before we receive God's forgiveness. That obedience means we must forgive others their wrongs to us in order to be forgiven.

Anger and Entitlement

It is impossible to grasp the idea of forgiveness without understanding anger. And it is impossible to feel anger without connecting the cause of the anger to real or perceived entitlement. When you think something ought to be yours, whether it really should be or not, you justify entitlement to the object. Another person, success, money, power, your personal property, an idea, a possession, personal space—all may be perceived to be rightfully yours. In other words, you feel entitled to them or perceive that you have a right to them. In reality, you are entitled to something only if you outright own it or if you have title to it by contract. You never own another person. You can't copyright ideas. Success is earned. Personal space is culturally defined.

When someone takes something or attempts to take something you believe to be yours by entitlement—or if someone else has something you feel should be yours by entitlement and they refuse to give it to you or it is impossible for them to do so—then anger results. When anger simmers, you become bitter. Often bitterness results in vengeful actions against your target. That is called revenge. When you are angry for a long period of time and let the hostility go untreated, depression can occur. Health risks also rise. High blood pressure, a reduced immune system, heart attacks, cancer, and any number of other maladies can overcome you if anger goes unchecked.

Road rage occurs frequently. Some people become so angry when they feel violated that they actually take out a gun and shoot someone. This definitely involves out-of-control emotions. Here the perpetrator's sense of entitlement is being put into play. For some reason, the driver has perceptually measured off personal space on the highway. When someone cuts in front of him and takes the space that driver assumes to be his, the driver cannot contain his hostility. In extreme cases, he may choose to shoot into the car that "stole his personal space." What a dreadful experience! How tragic that the shooter is so out of control of his emotions.

Several movies have been developed around the plot of an individual who falls in love with a person who doesn't reciprocate the affection. In fact, the love object never had any special feelings for the perpetrator. Maybe they were casual friends. Maybe they even went out on a date. But the love object never led the perpetrator to believe in any way that there was a love attraction involved. Here again, we have the dynamic of perceived entitlement coming into play. The perpetrator wants the love object but can't have her. He feels entitled to get what he wants. Anger arises. He stalks her. In watching her go out with other guys on dates, he is enraged. He tries to smear her reputation at the office. He continues to telephone her, trying to force her to go out with him. He becomes obsessed with her. Deep down, he wants to destroy her. Unless the stalker emotionally detaches from the target, big trouble may lie ahead.

In the case of Alan we have just studied, he felt that his relatives had taken away part of his life. He felt entitled to more free time from work for studying to make better grades for college qualification, to be able to pursue his dreams, and to have a less troublesome period during his youth. He interpreted his family's hardships as theft of his future. Alan became angry—very angry. His hostility negatively affected him for all of his adult life until he sought help. He evidently became a real jerk because of his bitterness. Until Alan forgave those whom he felt had taken away his future, he couldn't function well in life.

Forgiveness is not simple. Earlier in this chapter, we discussed Jesus' words to his disciples concerning the fact that they should forgive people who wronged them and had repented. That seems simple enough. Cause and effect are defined. A person wrongs someone else, the individual apologizes, is truly sorry for the behavior, and tries to do better. The victim of the wrongful behavior forgives her. All is well.

Most forgiveness episodes are not that easy. Many of the people who anger us have no idea how their behavior has affected us.

Maybe they are insensitive, emotionally unstable, suffer from borderline sociopathy with little or no empathy for others; or maybe they are simply ignorant of interpersonal communication. Therefore you will never receive an apology. Some people may be outright evil and never intend to apologize. If you remain angry at them, you are hurting only yourself by giving them control over your emotions and perhaps your physical health. You may need to move beyond the Biblical lessons we have shared earlier in this chapter and model after Joseph, whose story is told in Genesis 37-50.

Joseph, favorite son of Jacob, was sold into slavery by his jealous brothers and taken to Egypt. They lied to their father about Joseph's disappearance and thought they had disposed of Joseph forever. However, Joseph found favor with Egypt's Pharaoh and was put in charge of the Pharaoh's palace and all his people. Only the Pharaoh himself had more power. Finding himself governor of the land of Egypt, Joseph became very powerful in spite of ethnic differences between his Hebrew roots and the Egyptians he governed.

Many years later, there was a famine in their land, and Joseph's brothers were forced to go to Egypt to buy grain. And who did they encounter as governor? Yes, it was their brother Joseph. On their first trip, Joseph didn't tell them who he was. But later, when they returned for more grain, Joseph revealed his identity. I'm sure his brothers were frightened almost to death in expectation of revenge. In contrast, Joseph wept so loudly from joy that he could be heard in the next room. He held no grudge. He treated them well. He had forgiven their immense wrongdoing to him. Rather than be angry for their sin against him, Joseph felt that God had used the incident of his sale into slavery to put him in the right place at the right time.

It's all in our perception. When viewing injustices committed against us, whether or not we forgive depends on our perception of the situation. Joseph could have had his brothers killed for their dishonor. Instead he hugged them. On the cross, Jesus could have been furious with his persecutors. However, just the opposite was true. Jesus asked God to forgive them because of their situational ignorance; i.e., they didn't know what they were doing. If Jesus asked God to forgive his tormenters, then we will assume that Jesus had already forgiven them.

Joseph and Jesus never saw immediate repentance from their evildoers. Forgiveness came before repentance. Thus, the higher level of spiritual maturity for humanity is to perceive that the other person needs to be forgiven, then go ahead and do it. With the law of reciprocity at work, God will then extend grace to us in the same proportion (and even greater) when we need it. Forgiveness doesn't let people off the hook from consequences. If someone has committed a horrible crime, the victim will forgive him, but the guilty party will probably be forced to reap the consequences—perhaps serve a prison sentence or suffer an even worse consequence—based on the decision of a criminal jury or judge. Additionally, our extension of forgiveness does not indicate that we condone the perpetrator's behavior.

Forgiveness brings us peace. It doesn't necessarily remove earthly consequences. Only God can grant eternal forgiveness. Rather than view the individual as one from whom we must extract revenge, we can do the work of forgiveness and pacify our soul while limiting collateral damage to our other relationships. It is possible to change our perception from one of wrath to one of peace. We choose our perceptions of other people. We are then in charge of our resulting feelings, thus removing the control that others may have over us.

Ethnic, Racial, and Religious Anger

Hitler's Germany. Throughout history, evil rulers have inflicted harsh pain on their people. Corrupt tyrants have risen to power and practiced everything from rape and torture of their citizens to starving and killing them in order to keep the population subservient. That behavior is still taking place today in some countries. In these lands, life is cheap. People are angry but afraid to speak out. Citizens are depressed due to internalized hostility. Their lives seem hopeless.

I am a Baby Boomer who was born soon after World War II ended. As I matured, I was privy to many war stories from my relatives and friends who had experienced combat duty in Europe. Additionally, big box office attractions of the 1950s were movies depicting World War II heroes and starring such legends as Audie Murphy and John Wayne. Tugging at my emotions intensely, even as a small child, were stories of the atrocities committed by Adolf Hitler against the Jews. The cruel treatment inflicted upon these descendants of the ancient Hebrew people was incomprehensible.

Beginning in 1933, Hitler, Germany's supreme dictator, began his anti-Semitic campaign. According to reports from my Jewish friends, their relatives were restricted from holding jobs, not allowed to drive cars, stripped of their property, and denied their dignity. In his quest to conquer the entire world, Hitler did damage far and wide. One of his goals was to extinguish the life of every Jew on the globe. He managed to kill over 6,000,000 of them in what is now known as the Holocaust. That is estimated to be approximately one-third of the international Jewish population in the 1940s. Hitler boasted about his mass murders of the Jews. His followers would simultaneously kill hundreds of Jews in large gas chambers. Hitler gloated in the cruelty. Terror reigned.

American slavery. Before the American Revolution, people living in America held slaves from various ethnic and racial groups, many of whom were from Africa. Some of the slave owners were respectful of their servants; others were cruel. Even some of America's Founders owned slaves. Eventually, the moral values involved in slavery began to be questioned. The North was troubled by slavery and promoted freedom for its slaves. The agricultural South demanded intensive labor on the plantations and thus continued to promote slavery. Many of the slaves from the rural South managed to escape to the North and live in freedom. Christians helped many of them reach the North. A majority of the slaves, by the time of the Civil War in 1861, were African Americans. In 1863 the Emancipation Proclamation was issued by President Abraham Lincoln. This did not end slavery, however. Not until Amendment 13 to the U.S. Constitution was ratified in 1865 was slavery outlawed.

Yet African-American descendants of slaves continued to struggle, even in freedom, for a hundred years after their forefathers' enslavement. School segregation, unfair treatment by their communities, discrimination in the workplace, and general violations of their civil rights continued to take place. Rev. Dr. Martin Luther King, Jr. led a peaceful civil rights movement in the 1960s, bringing attention to the plight of African-American discrimination in the United States, especially in the South. Slowly, but surely, African Americans began to experience more equal opportunity than in the past.

South African apartheid. Racial segregation and white supremacy wreaked immense hardship on blacks in South Africa for several decades. Formally ending in 1991 as a result of economic pressures caused by international sanctions and protests from human rights activists, apartheid had oppressed people for at least two generations, perhaps more. As with post-slavery issues plaguing the United States during the 100 years after the U. S. Civil War, post-apartheid issues still scream for resolution in South Africa. Black poverty fuels anger over the division between the "haves and have-nots." Education of blacks in South Africa lags behind that of whites due to historically poor schooling and discrimination. Many whites live in opulence while a majority of the blacks exist in poverty. The economies of the two races differ radically.

Apartheid squeezed black people into a vice of extreme control. Although blacks outnumbered whites almost four to one in the population, white income compared to that of blacks had a fourteen to one ratio. In rural areas, the black infant mortality rate was 40 percent. (*The History of Apartheid in South Africa*, retrieved March 26, 2003, from http://www-cs-students.stanford.edu/~cale/cs201/apartheid.hist.html) Living under institutionalized racial discrimination, blacks had little, if any, opportunity for growth and development under the extreme conditions in South Africa from 1948 to 1991.

Ethnic, Racial, and Religious Forgiveness

Jewish acquaintances. Some of my elderly Jewish acquaintances have related to me the abject horror they felt as they watched their parents being marched off to the gas chambers. The fear, which later turned to hatred, remained with them for many years before coming to this country for a different life. One of them has indicated that she couldn't even utter the word "Germany" for many years without having a panic attack. Nightmares dominated her sleep patterns for two decades. Her loneliness ripped her soul. Life seemed so unfair.

African-American friends. As a child living on a North Texas farm, I had the opportunity to work beside African Americans who tended our fields and helped with the crops. Several families were employed by my father and lived in houses on our farm. The children and I spent many summer afternoons playing hide-and-seek and tag. As I grew older, I would spend long hours visiting with some of my African-American friends' mothers while the fathers were working with my dad either picking cotton, planting, or harvesting corn or wheat. They would tell me stories of their ancestors who were slaves.

By the time I had these conversations, four or five generations of African Americans had lived a life of freedom. My friends had deep sympathy for their forefathers and were grateful for the severe price they had paid for the future of their progeny. As I was growing up, however, I observed the distinct inequality of segregation. Many of the African Americans with whom I played as a child never attended school. When they went into town, they had to use water fountains and restrooms labeled "colored." My African-American friends rode in the backs of buses and ate at separate lunch counters. One day, I took my friend to a restaurant to eat lunch with me. The restaurant owner refused to serve us.

My African-American playmates worked the crops with their parents. As I grew older and the civil rights movement began, my conversations with them continued. I sensed something I had not noticed before—quiet anger. Much of the culture of my small Texas town reflected the values of the rural South (even though Texas is not considered to be in the deep South; rather, it is central to the South and Southwest). Until the 1960s, life seemed peaceful. Everyone assumed his "place" in society. Roles were clearly defined. Yet, looking back, I was too young to detect the degree to which many of my playmates and their parents were living lives of quiet desperation.

Apartheid survivors. In my travels, I have had the opportunity to meet victims of apartheid in South Africa. Before I studied the subject, I was astounded to hear about all the control to which the blacks were subjected. Their limitations were unbelievable. Their freedom was so restrained. The people would tell me of the suffering of their families back home and how they themselves had come to America to discover a better life. Their moods would shift from anger to depression over their family's plight.

When Nelson Mandella was released from prison after having served a long sentence for his stand against South African apartheid, I was asked to come to that country to participate in a ten-city tour while speaking on the future of freedom of all people in South Africa. I had too many schedule conflicts for the period of time required for my stay, and thus was unable to participate in the massive event. Of all the invitations I've had to turn down due to scheduling problems, I regretted most not being able to join that tour. When Mandella was released, something big was about to happen. I knew that. And I wanted to be a part of that sweeping change in South Africa's national consciousness. Years of oppression had damaged multi-generations. A wide gap existed between blacks and whites. Deep-seated anger abounded for lives restricted and opportunities lost.

Forgiving cruelty. Having seen firsthand the results of oppression handed down to the descendants of slaves, Jews executed by the Nazis, and South African apartheid, I can understand why forgiveness might be difficult. Ethnic anger is painful to overcome. Yet I have met people who have been victims of cruelty or whose ancestors suffered violent atrocities and have been able to forgive the perpetrators of evil. What is the difference between those who continue to hold a grudge and those who have been able to pardon the evildoers? The answer lies in their attitudes and perceptions fueled by Godly faith. Those who have forgiven their wrongdoers have chosen to do so.

Archbishop Desmond Tutu is known for his efforts to end apartheid in South Africa. For these struggles, he won the Nobel Peace Prize in 1984. In his book *No Future Without Forgiveness* (New York: Doubleday, 2000), he promotes healing of breached relationships. Archbishop Tutu was appointed by President Nelson Mandella to head the Truth and Reconciliation Commission created to look into all the violations committed under apartheid for the thirty-four-year period ending in 1994. Rather than promoting revenge for wrongs, Archibishop Tutu advocated forgiveness based on his belief that God created humanity to live in peace and harmony.

He differentiates between vengeful retributive justice and restorative justice, which heals broken relationships. It is obvious that Archbishop Tutu's philosophy of reconciliation is based on love and promotion of peace—much like the philosophy of Ghandi (who was influenced by Christianity) and Mother Teresa. Choosing to see the white perpetrators of wrongs against the blacks as people capable of living in harmony with blacks in a post-apartheid society, Archbishop Tutu stakes South Africa's future on the factor of forgiveness.

Restoring harmony. For communities and societies to restore peace after terrible ethnic and racial cruelty or religious conflict, forgiveness must take place. Although it is difficult, the memories of past abuses must be replaced with thoughts of present possibilities for harmony. Forgiveness is hard work. But it can happen. Everyone is capable of practicing forgiveness with God's help through the Holy Spirit.

Those individuals I know whose families, or even they themselves, have suffered ethnic, racial, or religious oppression, have learned to forgive the perpetrators, have been able to put the past behind them and live in the joy of today. Anger and hostility only rob us of the happiness we can experience now. We can never redeem the past, but we can make an investment in the present. By so doing, we can then fabricate a fruitful future.

Learning to Forgive

Without forgiveness, anger and bitterness control us. In fact, Mark 11:25 emphatically states that when we pray, we should get rid of anger against all people so that God can forgive us. According to that passage, God's forgiveness of us is related to our forgiveness of others. Recognizing that forgiveness involves concerted and deliberate effort, I have developed a model for the forgiveness process. Application of this paradigm can renew your life.

Step 1—Decide to forgive. Forgiveness begins with a decision to change your way of thinking about another person or situation. By the time you have reached this decision, often the pain has become uncomfortable. The anger you feel is distracting you from the more pleasant aspects of life. Your health may be negatively affected. Perhaps your relationships with your friends and family are becoming strained because you are obsessed with past hurts and anger. Whatever the case, something will trigger your decision. That stimulus will begin the arduous process of forgiveness.

Step 2—Formulate a scenario of the hurtful situation. Revisit the past hurt and create a story about the events, people, and circumstances that caused your anger. Record your story in a journal. Communicate it to trusted friends or counselors. Your story will have at least two characters: the perceived perpetrator of the hurt and the victim. Allow your listener or reader of the story to question you about specifics of your case. Answer them honestly without putting up defenses. Be open to questioning as a forum for learning.

Step 3—Search for entitlements. Recalling our earlier discussion of anger's relationship to entitlement, we saw that anger derives either from: (a) someone taking something that we feel entitled to; or (b) someone possessing something we feel entitled to and that person will not or cannot give it to us. In other words, someone takes something from us we don't want them to have, or we want something from another person that the individual won't or can't give us. Either situation triggers an angry response. Entitlement, then, is a feeling that we have a right to something.

At this stage, it is important to analyze your story in order to define your entitlements. Ask yourself if your feeling of entitlement is justified. For example, in a child kidnapping case, parents will feel anger because something they feel entitled to has been taken from them. A gift from God, their precious child, specifically entrusted to these parents for safekeeping, has been stolen from them. Although parents do not own their children, they are charged to be good stewards of the child's spiritual and physical growth and development. The child has a right to parental protection. The entitlement is real. The anger is real.

Another example involves jealousy, which Paul decries in Galatians 5:20. Gene is the youngest of four children. There were eleven years between the time he was born and when his older brother came into the world. His family was so excited by Gene's arrival that they gave him lots of attention. The older children took him everywhere with them. His parents favored him and offered him every opportunity they could afford. Since the family was of middle-class status, money was usually tight and had to be closely budgeted. Gene grew up with three friends whose individual family incomes were substantially greater than the income of Gene's family. With access to more money, the friends could drive flashier cars than Gene could afford. Their clothes were more fashionable, and their homes were more lavishly furnished. After associating with people who had more wealth, Gene decided that he would excel in school, acquire advanced degrees, and become affluent in early adulthood.

Gene worked hard in school and graduated in the top ten percent of his class. He excelled academically in college. He was also a leader in various campus activities. Upon graduation, Gene was offered several lucrative jobs. He chose a sales position with a major global company in order to earn a sizable income and purchase all the luxuries he had always wanted. However, Gene had not calculated the heavy competition in the sales field. There was constant pressure to produce more; and Gene was willing to do what it took to earn substantial money. He began to feel stressed much of the time. Work became less exciting. He began to suffer burnout. After ten years of hard-driving ambition, he had a light heart attack at thirty-five years of age. He took stock of his life and decided to change careers. Yet he still felt that he deserved the material things he had always wanted.

Gene secured a position that paid less money than his sales commissions had brought him. He had more career peace of mind, and his on-the-job stress was reduced. Yet he frequently felt a sense of emotional churning. Anger alternated with depression. He became confused about his feelings. When Jason, his best friend, purchased a new expensive car, he acted happy on the outside, but he was angry on the inside. When someone would comment to Gene about how well Jason was doing in his career, Gene would find something negative to say about Jason. Deep down, he wanted to hurt Jason. Then Jason married a lovely lady, and they built a marvelous house. Gene fumed at the thought of Jason's happiness. He pretended to be happy for Jason, but he wasn't. He began to sabotage Jason by telling his other close friends some things that Jason had shared with him in confidence.

Then the internal anger turned to depression. Gene became so depressed that he didn't want to see anyone socially anymore. He just worked, came home, and watched TV. He felt as if he were a loser when comparing his wealth to Jason's. He spent a lot of time mentally competing with Jason. Finally, Gene became so miserable that he went to a counselor to determine why he was so angry at Jason. The counselor helped Gene conclude that he was jealous of Jason's success. Jealousy is a form of anger that happens when we feel entitled to acquire for ourselves something another person has. Someone might be jealous of another's success, happiness, material possessions, family, friends—or any number of things. Deep down, Gene didn't want Jason to have wealth and happiness because Gene's income had been reduced, and he wasn't happy.

Gene's sense of entitlement is misplaced. It is not real. He was wrong to feel anger toward Jason. Gene needed to work through his own needs and quit projecting blame onto Jason. Jealousy is harmful and is evoked by erroneous emotional entitlement.

Step 4—Take action. Various health maladies and distressful emotional reactions occur if a person is stuck in anger and hostility for a long period of time. While in a state of "stuckness," the victim becomes obsessed with getting even and often plots revenge. When an individual allows another party to have this much control over his mind, much of the joy available to him in the present drains from his life. The cost of such emotional attachment to the past is immense.

Action is demanded in order for physical and emotional health to be restored. The victim of anger must mentally detach from the person who angered her. She must arrive at the point where thoughts of this person do not cause her any emotional stress. She must neutralize the person and the past situation in her life. This neutralization process will happen when she learns to emotionally detach and grieve the loss. During this step, it is important to think positively that there is something better on the other side of this pain. The Bible assures Christians that sorrow is temporary. Happiness eventually returns. (Psalm 30:5)

In the case of Gene cited above, it is important that he understands the cause of his jealousy and takes action to find his own personal worth through Jesus Christ. Consulting a counselor was a great first step. A Christian counselor can help him determine his true God-defined purpose in life. His self-esteem is being defined by externals, and he suffers from greed. Gene must forgive himself. He must let go of his futile quest for his illusion of happiness. His compelling ambition for material possessions nearly killed him when he had his heart attack. By assessing his God-given purpose in life, Gene will eventually be able to find true contentment and realize how delusive the quest for material possessions becomes. He can make actionable plans for detaching from external rewards and begin finding gratification in eternal dividends.

Step 5—Exercise conscious choices. During the forgivenenss process, please remember that you have choices. Here are a few of those choices that you can exercise. It is a good idea to mentally rehearse some or all of these statements as you undergo the demanding work of forgiveness.

- I can choose to put God first in my life and not expect perfection from other people or myself.
- I can choose to disempower my negative memories and thoughts.

- I can choose to view a hurtful situation in the past as part of God's plan for my life knowing that He turns hurts into helps.
- I can choose to view my situation differently by allowing the Holy Spirit to transform my mind.
- I can choose to give up my anger and the need for revenge.
- I can choose to see positives for personal growth.
- I can choose not to judge the other person's motives and leave that judgment to God.
- I can choose to believe that the past does not repeat itself.
- I can choose to draw healthy boundaries between my life now and my life in the past.
- I can choose to follow the two great commandments of Jesus Christ (Mark 12:30-31): love God with all my being; love others equal to myself.
- I can choose to forgive, to pardon, and to taste joy again.

Step 6—Move forward. Don't look back. Jesus was adamant about moving forward. As a result, He said that a person who looks back isn't deserving of His kingdom. (Luke 9:62) Fill your life with new people and activities.

Forgiveness doesn't necessarily involve reconciliation. It does not mean that you must have a renewed relationship with the perceived perpetrator of the wrong against you or that you condone his behavior. Forgiveness involves emotional detachment and letting go of your anger against another person. Of course, if reconciliation happens, that would be wonderful. However, it may not happen. Thus it is necessary to put the situation behind you and move toward a positive future.

When your life is filled with exciting adventures and new people, eventually you can neutralize old hurts. Growth in your spiritual maturity enables you to concentrate on giving rather than getting. Then you can live a revitalized life.

Your Future, Your Choice

Throughout God's plan for humanity, He has always provided a positive perspective. When destruction happened, there was always a remnant of His people left to rebuild. Today, there is invariably something good awaiting Christians who are willing to forgive. All we need is the faith to endure and the fortitude to work with the Holy Spirit in taking positive action for a favorable future. By planning our actions in tandem with God's wishes, He guarantees our future success. (Proverbs 16:3) As Christians forgive, God forgives.

CHAPTER 8
God Will Heal Our Land

*Christians can expect God through
Jesus Christ to make our nation
spiritually whole again if we obey Him.*

The last of God's three promises in 2 Chronicles 7:14 was to heal the land. In the Old Testament, God promised to restore their nation if His people would meet His four requirements. The land frequently suffered physical damage in the form of droughts, devastation from locusts, famines, and wars—to name a few disasters. God would then renew their land to productivity. There were good times and bad, feasts and famines, wars and peace, great crop yields and near starvation. When God's people were focused on Him and obedient, He restored their nation. After Solomon had finished building the temple, God told him that if He chose to bring hardship on Israel, He would remove the difficulty and restore Israel to health and productivity if the Israelites would: humble themselves before Him, pray, seek His presence, and repent of their sins.

That verse still holds true. Christians, through Jesus Christ, are God's people today just as the Israelites were God's chosen people in the Old Testament. Presently, Christians can expect God through Jesus Christ to make our nation spiritually whole again if we will obey Him. In the New Testament, Jesus Christ is a spiritual savior (or healer).

Because Jesus was no longer physically on earth, God sent a Protector, Counselor, and Comforter to be with His people. We know Him as the Holy Spirit, who promises to get us through any situation according to God's will. (John 14:15-20) Christ's kingdom is supernatural, not physical. However, when Christians are spiritually whole, they are resting in the protection of Jesus Christ, who resides inside them in the form of the Holy Spirit. Thus they are under God's shelter. (Psalm 91)

If God's people, in humility, will turn back to Him, pray, confess their sins, and turn away from their wrongdoings, He will physically protect America according to the will of God. Some ways by which God physically protects His people are through

- providing capable individuals with innovative ideas for: defense and security technology; detecting, preventing, and curing diseases; and thwarting terrorist attacks through accurate intelligence-gathering;
- inspiring people to protect one another;
- creating opportunities for learning and education;
- motivating people to acquire higher education and perform their vocations with excellence;
- shaping seemingly serendipitous conditions for success;
- communicating warning signals through people's thoughts and instincts;
- causing the enemy to have "bad luck";
- performing humanly unexplainable miracles.

I have observed as I have read this scripture from many translations and reviewed several commentaries that obedience must be a way of life. These four requirements are most effective for God's maximum protection when they are ongoing and not quickly activated in a last desperate attempt to be rescued from harm. When the destruction is already in progress, greater loss will occur—although God doesn't preclude saving us in the last moment if our pleas and repentance are sincere. He is all-powerful and can deliver His people at any time from any disaster.

America Is Hurting

For a nation to be healed, we must assume that it is hurting.

Numerous studies of American life during the last several years indicate that, indeed, this assumption is true. If Christians allow God to remedy their pain, they can have intimate experiences with Him and learn to rely on His plans for their lives. If, however, Christians pursue their own self-centered cures for their maladies, they will take paths that will lead them away from God. Those avenues involve sin and destruction.

According to a variety of surveys, a great majority of Americans consider themselves to be Christians. If America is hurting, then Christians are hurting. Increasingly, happenings in the world at large are being reflected in the church. For example, the divorce rate of Christians is equal to or greater than that of all Americans. To a great extent, then, Christians reflect the values and behavior of everyone in America.

In their book *The Social Health of the Nation: How America Is Really Doing* (New York, Oxford: Oxford University Press, 1999), sociologists Marc Miringoff of Fordham University and Marque-Luisa Miringoff of Vassar College show that America's social health has dropped substantially since the early 1970s. Their data are derived from administration of their widely respected Index of Social Health, which they originated in the early 1970s and continue to release annually.

According to an MSNBC news report in December 1999, Prozac prescriptions were being written by doctors at a rate eleven times that of seven years earlier. CNN news media reported in February 2000 that Russia and the United States lead the world in sexually transmitted diseases. They also noted during the same newscast that anorexia cases grew by 1,000 times in the five-year period before the year 2000. All this misery and pain were being felt during one of the best economic periods America had ever experienced. The facts are very telling: wealth does not necessarily produce peace and happiness. People are definitely hurting. Further, it appears that people are looking for cures to emotional and spiritual pain in all the wrong places. Their souls are definitely in need (SIN). Remember our SIN acrostic in Chapter 5? If not, you might want to review that chapter at this point.

With global chaos and economic uncertainty pressing on people's lives, individuals are reporting high levels of stress. Instead of turning to God for answers, they are turning to alcohol, drugs, workaholism (including paid and/or volunteer work), anger, revenge, conflict, pornography, relationship addictions, and overeating or undereating as a few of their outlets. These self-directed cures for people's needs can damage their bodies and cause casualties in collateral relationships. Child and spousal abuse abound. Youth suicides and homicides are making news headlines too often.

The percentage of drug abuse cases in America is more than double what it was in the 1970s. MSNBC News reported in 2001 that the United States has five percent of the world's population and consumes 50 percent of the world's illicit drugs. Global AIDS is rampant, threatening to wipe out a large percentage of whole generations in some countries. Child poverty is worse in the United States than in most civilized countries and ranks above American elderly poverty, thereby causing children to be at a competitive disadvantage even before they have had a chance to live many years of life. The rich/poor gap is growing wider, thus disenfranchising many people from mainstream society. All this comes at a time when the U.S. budget is tight, there is worldwide ideological unrest, and a prolonged war on terrorism. Greater portions of the U.S. budget will be directed to homeland and global security needs, thus curbing governmental help to the poor, socially marginalized, and spiritually bankrupt. Faith-based groups and non-profit social agencies will assume more responsibility for helping people whose souls are in distress.

Samplings of the portion of Baby Boomers born from 1946 through 1954 and the segment of Generation Y born from 1975 through 1994 were studied to find out what percentage of the respondents in each of these two groups felt that most people in their age group they knew came from "loving, stable" families. Compared to their counterparts in other major countries, those two groups studied in the United States ranked very low. (Pamela Paul, "Global Generation Gap," based on "Generations and Gaps" conducted by InsightExpress for Euro RSCG Worldwide, from *American Demographics,* March 2002, pages 18-19) Another study by Don Peck and Ross Douthat investigated the work of Dutch sociologist Ruut Neenhoven through the 1990s. His studies indicate that the United States is not the happiest nation in the world even though it is extremely wealthy by world standards. Such nations as Nicaragua, Iceland, and Luxembourg rank higher than the United States in happiness even though they are poorer. (*Atlantic Monthly*, January/February 2003, pages 42-23) Seemingly, after one attains a certain degree of wealth, money doesn't buy happiness. Interesting observation!

Considering the aggregate of statistics cited in the previous paragraphs, it becomes obvious that in spite of living in a wealthy country and the only superpower nation on earth, people in America are spiritually hungry. They are searching as never before for soul satisfaction. People have approached me after some of my seminars and speeches on this topic and told me that they actually ache inside. While living in their large house with a beautifully landscaped lawn, owning two expensive automobiles plus a recreational vehicle, dining in fine restaurants, taking exotic vacations, and having a wonderful, healthy family, they long for a simpler, slower lifestyle. They wish for more time with family, peace of mind, closer bonding with one another, less stress, and time to contemplate a sunrise while slowly savoring a cup of flavorful coffee. What they are telling me is that they wish for eternal wealth. They have material riches. Their spiritual well is dry. Their eternal account is bankrupt.

Diagnosis: Misplaced Faith

Faith is reliance upon something we perceive to be trustworthy. That in which we place our ultimate trust becomes our god. Before going any further with this discussion, it will be helpful if you will fill out the following inventory.

Place a check mark by the statements that pertain to you.

_____ I feel that God is distant most of the time.

_____ I communicate with God only when I need something from Him.

_____ I pray to God only after I've exhausted all other potential avenues of fulfillment.

_____ If I were really truthful with myself, I'd say that I place my trust for future security in my cash and investments more than in God.

_____ My emotional security lies in other people.

_____ I believe that the United States can dominate in any war be-

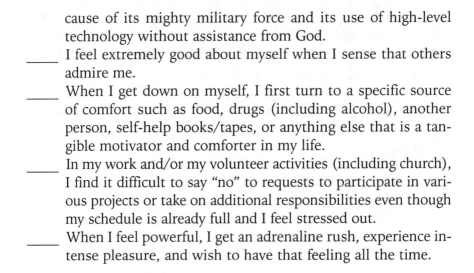

cause of its mighty military force and its use of high-level technology without assistance from God.

_____ I feel extremely good about myself when I sense that others admire me.

_____ When I get down on myself, I first turn to a specific source of comfort such as food, drugs (including alcohol), another person, self-help books/tapes, or anything else that is a tangible motivator and comforter in my life.

_____ In my work and/or my volunteer activities (including church), I find it difficult to say "no" to requests to participate in various projects or take on additional responsibilities even though my schedule is already full and I feel stressed out.

_____ When I feel powerful, I get an adrenaline rush, experience intense pleasure, and wish to have that feeling all the time.

Count the number of check marks. By checking one or more of the above statements, you are indicating a tendency to trust other sources than God for anesthetizing your hurts and fulfilling your needs. The more check marks you made, the less you put your ultimate faith in God. Please use the following guidelines for insight.

1-3 check marks: Minimal use of self-centered life-solutions, although even a score of "1" indicates a tendency to misplace your trust.

4-6 check marks: Moderate use of material crutches; habitual creation of other gods; frequently misplaced trust.

7-10 check marks: High level of misplaced trust; definite and repeated creation of other gods in your life; focus trending away from God-trust; likelihood of personal hurt, stress, disappointment, and frustration.

This is not a scientific survey, so please take it only as an indicator of your degree of misplaced trust. Additionally, this instrument does not exhaust every possibility of gods we create for ourselves. Hopefully, however, it will be helpful to you in determining whether you are focusing on the one true God through Jesus Christ for placing your ultimate confidence. Trusting other gods violates the first of the Ten Commandments (Exodus 20:3) and the first of Jesus' two commandments (Matthew 22:37).

When we trust anyone or anything above God, we set ourselves up for disappointment. The idea is to think big by trusting in God above all else. We must think beyond our own capacity. By seeking God's guidance when setting goals, making plans, and tapping necessary resources, we are able to experience real power and security. God will provide us with capabilities and protection that are only available through His supernatural eternal existence.

Our Faith Initiates God's Guarantee

Often I write a whole book before deciding on its title. However, with this book, I knew the title immediately after reading 2 Chronicles 7:14, the scripture central to this work. It was so obvious that if God's people met the four requirements God revealed to Solomon, then God would keep His three promises to Israel. That was God's guarantee—hence the title of this book. As I wrote this work over several weeks, the direction I was to take was revealed to me as needed. Now, toward the end, the path has led to the topic of faith. Upon review of Hebrews 11:1 to determine the definition of the word *faith,* which in part means the "substance of things hoped for," I discovered that *substance* means *guaranty,* or *guarantee,* in the type of Greek applied by some authors of the New Testament. (James Orr, M.A., D.D. General Editor, "Faith," *International Standard Bible Encyclopedia,* 1915, www.studylight.org/enc/isb/view.cgi?number=T3349)

I was totally astounded to find where this long journey was leading. Our faith in Jesus Christ guarantees our hopes. Amazing! That's what the writer of Hebrews meant. All Christ requires of us is our utmost, priority-number-one faith. We are to have such blind faith in Him that we know beyond the shadow of a doubt that He will keep His promises to us if we trust Him. He will fulfill all our God-focused hopes and dreams if we will give Him our undivided faith. John 3:16 indicates that all who have faith in Jesus Christ will have eternal life.

In order to meet the four requirements in God's promise to Solomon, we must have faith. Only ultimate faith made possible by the Holy Spirit would cause us to humble ourselves, pray, seek God above all else, and turn from our self-prescribed solutions to focus on Him for our salvation and protection. Our faith causes God to heal us. The steadfast faith of Christians in America will cause God to heal our nation.

What Is Faith?

We hear a lot these days about faith-based initiatives and faith-based institutions. In these cases, faith pertains to religion or creed more than utmost trust and reliance. Many people believe that faith is all about religious rules and doctrine, about living according to the dictates of pious people who pass judgment on our behavior. Many people have attended legalistic churches that taught religion and faith together as similar in definition. As a result, numerous folks felt bored, disappointed, and frustrated by their inability to live up to the standards set for them. They are now likely to be unchurched.

However, religion and faith are very different. Christian faith involves taking our trust and placing it fully in Jesus Christ, thereby establishing an intimate, living, loving, close relationship with Him through a vital Holy Spirit that comes to reside in our innermost being (heart). In order to do that, we must first have recognized and acknowledged that we are sinful humans, as all are, and capable of mistakes. We declare our imperfections. (Romans 3:23) We then decide to shift our faith from this material world and self to reliance on God through Jesus Christ. At that moment, something supernatural happens. We enter eternal life never to leave again. We then have access to God's power, wisdom, unconditional love, hope, and plans for our life through the Holy Spirit. The holes in our soul are in the process of being filled God's way—not our way.

Spiritual Maturity

The initial placing of our ultimate faith in God through Jesus Christ does not guarantee an instant solution to all our soul-needs. It is only the beginning of a transformation process that will last throughout life. God's ultimate goal for every Christian is Christlikeness. God matures our faith through: challenging life circumstances; making good things happen from negative situations even though He did not cause them; and disciplining us when we wander away from our God-focus into self-focus. He remains loyal and present in our lives for comfort, inspiration, and motivation through the Holy Spirit.

After we place our faith in God and make Him the Leader of our life, the next thing we should do is to read His Manual of Operations that He inspired authors to record. That Roadmap of Life is the Bible.

By reading it repeatedly and studying it deeply, God's character and expectations will be obvious. Many people tell me that the Bible is just a collection of ancient stories and is not relevant to life today. Wrong! I have been studying the Bible all my life, and it is as relevant today as it was many years ago. When I read modern translations of the Bible, it is amazing how true-to-life that collection of wisdom becomes. Answers to life's big dilemmas are housed in the Holy scriptures.

It is also helpful to realize that God is in control of your life if you are a Christian. Nothing is an accident. Even if God didn't cause something to happen to you, He for some reason didn't stop it. He allowed it. Therefore it's part of His plan for your life. When bad things happen, He can turn them into good things for the long term if you have ultimate faith in Him. When I get frustrated and disappointed because I didn't get something I wanted, I stop to think—often much later—that God has other plans for me and that I must wait patiently for the next step. Wow, is that sometimes hard for me to do!

God is in control of our life's master plan; but we are in charge of our day-to-day choices, although I believe God directs those choices if we consult Him. When our decisions bring negative consequences, we should be willing to experience those outcomes while assessing how we can grow from the circumstances. We can trust God to maneuver those negative outcomes and create positives for us in His ultimate plan. The important issue is that we have learned from our experiences and have faced the truth about ourselves.

Faith Is Actionable

Faith is not passive. To demonstrate the concept, James indicated that without action, faith is stagnant. (James 2:14-18) Jesus said that if we have faith, even as small as a tiny mustard seed—and mustard seeds are indeed tiny—we can cause heavy mountains to move. (Matthew 17:20-21) Just *thinking* about moving mountains or changing the world isn't enough. Having faith means accomplishing what, at first, might seem impossible. We must put our God-ideas into action. We then activate our faith.

A family inventor. My dad's cousin took the mustard-seed scripture literally approximately sixty years ago. He wanted to move mountains so that highways could go through them. Thus he invented a machine that would drill through hard rock. Roads were cut through many mountain passes into ski resorts that otherwise might not have been there so soon. My relative dared to put his belief into action. He had no money to invest in his idea, so he actively recruited investors. After that, he manufactured and sold the machines. He also had many other inventions during his creative and productive career.

By believing something can happen and praying to God for the wisdom and energy to make it happen, He will inspire us with ways to find the resources for directing positive outcomes—if our vision fits God's will. When you believe that God wants you to accomplish something, go for it! Do it! He will clear the way for you. (Proverbs 16:3) Often people set their own goals and ask God to bless them. Maybe He will, maybe He won't. God wants us to first seek His guidance for establishing our objectives and plans, then He will bless them abundantly. (Psalm 37:4)

Noah, the boat builder. Noah walked closely with God on a regular basis. One day, God told Noah that He was going to destroy the world by a flood. To save himself, his family, and a sampling of animals, Noah was told by God to build a large boat (ark). God even gave him the exact specifications. Noah obeyed. He worked on the ark for many years. Can you imagine what the neighbors thought—a man building an ark to prepare for a flood in a dusty, arid land? They must have laughed and joked at Noah's craziness. But the flood did come. The earth's people were destroyed—all except Noah, his family, and the animals he had preserved (Genesis 5-9).

Abraham, Father of the Jews. A childless wanderer, Abraham, was chosen by God to head a nation. But first, God told him to leave his homeland and follow His orders. Abraham heard God's voice and trusted Him. He set out for Canaan, a land that his descendants would possess. He followed God's instructions. Wandering off the righteous path at times, trying to do things his own way, even lying, Abraham would always come back to the way God was making for him. God promised him and his elderly wife, Sarah, children. And God delivered that pledge in His own time. The birth of children to elderly couples seemed physically impossible. But God created a miracle as He often does.

After many generations passed, Jesus was born. He came down through the lineage of Abraham. Dying before possessing Canaan,

Abraham was a link in God's chain. Through Abraham, known as the Father of the Jews, a great nation was built and all the world was blessed. Abraham didn't live to see it. However, by trusting God, Abraham changed the world!

Sometimes when we step out on faith and take action, we may not see the outcome. We must be content to be a part of God's master plan. He may be using us as a stepping stone. In following God, we must be faithful and trust that we have joined Him in creating His big picture for humanity.

Jeremiah, the investor. When Judah was under siege by Babylon, the prophet Jeremiah sensed God telling him to buy a piece of property in his war-torn land. Never mind that the Jews were being overrun and were ready to be taken into Babylonian captivity for a great number of years. Judah was devastated. God's idea made no human sense. But God inspired Jeremiah to believe that someday his homeland would be restored. So he stepped out in confidence and purchased some property. (Jeremiah 32:9) That's faith in action! And we know the rest of the story: The Jews were exiled but eventually a remnant of them did return to their land. Jeremiah had made a wise investment!

Role models. By studying the faith of Noah, Abraham, and Jeremiah, as well as many other heroes of the Bible, we can grasp the sacrifice that comes with faith. When we believe in God and trust Him, we follow His instructions. Some of the demands are great. Many of the actions we must take are hard. But God refines us and builds character so that we are continually up to the task.

In taking action for God, think big. Pursue eternal things, then the material blessings will follow as byproducts. With God's wisdom, pursue dreams and goals that are too big to imagine without God's help. If you don't need God, then your dreams and resulting actions are too small. Godly faith is actionable. It causes us to create grand visions and accomplish magnificent goals.

Hope and a Future

God told Jeremiah that he had plans for him: to give him hope and provide a successful future. (Jeremiah 29:11) The same message holds true today. God has opened His invitation worldwide among all people to join Him in His global work. Christians are

God's people. America's restoration begins with activation of our country's Christian faith. A wonderful future awaits the United States of America when her Christians humble themselves to God; come to Him in earnest prayer; fervently seek Him; then examine their lives and turn from focus on self-centered pursuits to their Godly mission.

The United States has never experienced such greatness and progress as will be possible when our nation's Christians (reportedly almost eight out of ten Americans) actualize their Godly faith. I envision an America wherein the following is possible:

Human life will be respected. Hurts emanating from hate will be healed. Our homeland will be secure. Healthy conflicts will be managed. People will pursue excellence. Motives will be pure. Relationships will thrive. Lives will be happy. People's word will be their bond. All children will thrive.

The elderly will be safe in their homes. The poor will not go hungry. Crime will be rare. Innovative ideas will flourish. Arrogance will diminish. People will respect one another. Love will abound. The nation will be prosperous. "In God We Trust" will continue to be our motto. Our cities will again be unstained by human tears. God will protect and bless us. No force can defeat us.

This hopeful vision for our country is from my very human perspective. Only God knows exactly how the healing will happen. But we do know that God keeps His promises. If America's Christians will heed His requirements, He will, in His own time and in His own way, heal our land.

That's God's guarantee to America!